Take Notes

2nd Edition

R

CAREER PRESS
180 Fifth Avenue
P.O. Box 34
Hawthorne, NJ 07507
1-800-CAREER-1
201-427-0229 (outside U.S.)
FAX: 201-427-2037

TAKE NOTES (2ND ED.)

ISBN 1-56414-076-8, $6.95

Cover design by A Good Thing, Inc.

Printed in the U.S.A. by Book-mart Press

To order this title by mail, please include price as noted above, $2.50 handling per order, and $1.00 for each book ordered. Send to: Career Press, Inc., 180 Fifth Ave., P.O. Box 34, Hawthorne, NJ 07507.

Or call toll-free 1-800-CAREER-1 (Canada: 201-427-0229) to order using VISA or MasterCard, or for further information on books from Career Press.

Library of Congress Cataloging-in-Publication Data

Fry, Ronald W.
    Take notes / by Ron Fry. -- 2nd ed.
        p.   cm.
    Includes index.
    ISBN 1-56414-076-8
    1. Note-taking.   I. Title.
LB2395.25.F78   1994
371.3'028'12--dc20   94-5491
                                                CIP

Table of

CONTENTS

WHO IS THIS BOOK *REALLY* FOR?

All of the now-seven titles in my **HOW TO STUDY Program** were originally written, or so I thought at the time, for high school students. But over the years I've discovered that the students buying these books are either already in college (which says wonderful things about the preparation they got in high school), in junior high (which says something much more positive about their motivation and, probably, eventual success) or returning to college (about whom more later).

Many of you reading this are adults. Some of you are returning to school. And some of you are long out of school but have figured out that if you could learn *now* the study skills your teachers never taught you, you'll do better in your careers.

All too many of you are parents with the same lament: "How do I get Johnny (Janie) to do better in school? He (she) should be getting As but seems to be happy getting Cs."

So I want to briefly take the time to address every one of the audiences for this book and discuss some of the factors particular to each of you:

If you're a high school student

You should be particularly comfortable with both the language and format of the book—its relatively short sentences and paragraphs, occasionally humorous (hopefully) headings and subheadings, a reasonable but certainly not outrageous vocabulary. I wrote it with you in mind!

If you're a junior high school student

You are trying to learn how to study at *precisely* the right time. Sixth, seventh and eighth grades—before that sometimes cosmic leap to high school—is without a doubt the period in which all these study skills should be mastered, since doing so will make high school not just easier but a far more positive and successful experience. Although written for high school-level readers, if you're serious enough about studying to be reading this book, I doubt you'll have trouble with the concepts or the language. You're probably just getting to classes where good, serious note-taking is important, so your timing is impeccable!

If you're a "traditional" college student

...somewhere in the 18 to 25 age range, I would have hoped you had already mastered most if not all of the basic study skills, especially note-taking. Since you haven't, please make learning, using and mastering all of the study skills covered in my **HOW TO STUDY** *Program* an absolute priority. Do not pass "Go." Do not go on a date. Take the time to learn these skills now. You may have been able to slide by in high school with mediocre note-taking skills, for example. I suspect you'll find college is another world, one in which you'll find yourself "sliding" down the grading curve unless you get serious about your study skills...right now!

If you're the parent of a student of any age

You must be convinced of one incontestable fact: It is highly unlikely that your child's school is doing anything to teach him or her how to study. Yes, of course they should. Yes, I know that's what you thought you paid taxes for. Yes, yes, yes. But, but, but—believe me, *they're not doing it.*

How do I know? For one thing, in thousands of interviews on radio, TV and in the print media, my publisher has allowed me to make the same offer: They will give any teacher or school administrator wishing to use any or all of the books in my **HOW TO STUDY *Program*** one *free* book for every one they purchase. That's right, buy 10, get 10 free. Buy 100, get 100 free.

There are three teachers out there—all three spending *their own money*, mind you—who have taken me up on that offer. Says something about priorities, doesn't it?

I also spend a lot of time talking to students and visiting schools. And the lack of study skills training is woefully obvious, whether the school is in the poorest section of town or the richest, in the inner city or suburban heaven, public or private, elementary, junior high or high school.

Note-taking in particular is one of the skills many teachers seem to assume students can simply learn by osmosis, since so few of them spend even a day teaching the rudiments of taking pertinent, accurate notes. And it is one of the skills that *you* can definitely and easily help your child master, even if you have to master it yourself first.

Take Notes

Don't for a minute underestimate the importance of *your* commitment to your child's success: Your involvement in your child's education is absolutely essential to his or her eventual success. Surprisingly enough, the results of every study done in the last two decades about what affects a child's success in school concludes that only one factor *overwhelmingly* affects it, every time: parental involvement. Not the size of the school, the money spent per pupil, the number of language labs, how many of the student body go on to college, how many great teachers there are (or lousy ones). All factors, yes. *But none as significant as the effect **you** can have.*

So please, take the time to read this book (and all of the others in the series, but especially **How to Study**) yourself. Learn what your kids *should* be learning. (And which of the other five subject-specific books in the series your child needs the most.)

And you can help tremendously, *even if you were not a great student yourself, even if you never learned great study skills.* You can learn now together with your child—not only will it help him or her in school, it will help *you* on the job, whatever your job.

Even if you think you need help only in a single area—or two or three—don't use only the specific book in my program that highlights that subject. Read **How to Study** first, *all the way through.* First of all, it will undoubtedly help you increase your mastery of skills you thought you already had. And it will cover those you need help with in a more concise manner. With that background, you will get *more* out of whichever of the other six books you use.

Presuming you need all the help all seven books can give you, what order should you read them in? Aside from reading **How to Study** first—all the way through—I don't think it matters. All of the study skills are interrelated, so practicing one already helps you with the others. If pushed, however, I will admit that I would probably suggest **Improve Your Reading** and **Manage Your Time** be the first two books you study. The former because reading is the basis of every other study skill, the latter because organization is the foundation on which the study pyramid is erected. After that, take your pick!

If you're a nontraditional student

If you're going back to high school, college or graduate school at age 25, 45, 65 or 85—you probably need the help these seven books offer more than anyone! Why? Because the longer you've been out of school, the more likely you don't remember what you've forgotten. And you've forgotten what you're supposed to remember! As much as I emphasize that it's rarely too early to learn good study habits, I must also emphasize that it's never too *late*.

Why you're holding a new edition

I first wrote **How to Study** in 1988, convinced that schools were doing a lousy job of teaching kids how to study— synonymous, to me, with teaching them how to *learn*—and that no one was picking up the slack. (I was also convinced—and still am—that most kids wanted *desperately* to learn but would, without some help, find it easier to fail. And failure, once welcomed, is a nasty habit to break.)

Published in 1989, most bookstores wedged one or two copies of **Study** in between the hundreds of phone book-sized test prep volumes. Career Press wasn't a big enough publisher to convince the "chains"—Waldenbooks, Barnes & Noble, B. Dalton—to stock it in any quantity or rich enough to spend any money promoting it.

Take Notes

Need will out. Tens of thousands of people who obviously needed **How to Study** ferreted out copies wherever they lurked and bought them. In 1990, the chains—who *are* smart enough to at least spot a winner the *second* time around—bought 6-copy "prepacks" and gave the book a little more prominence. (Meaning you didn't have to get a hernia removing other books to find a copy of **Study**.) Career Press sent me around the country to appear on radio and TV, including CNN. And hundreds of newspapers and magazines noticed what we were doing and started writing about **How to Study**. (The fact that test scores had declined for the hundred-fortieth year in a row or so probably had something to do with this, but who am I to quibble with the attention?)

In 1991, *booksellers* started calling to say they hoped I was planning some follow-up books to **Study**. And hundreds of parents and students wrote or called to indicate they needed more help in some specific areas. **Ron Fry's HOW TO STUDY Program** was born, featuring a second edition of **Study** and four new books—**Improve Your Reading, Manage Your Time, Take Notes and Write Papers**—that delved even deeper into critical study skills. That year I spent more time on the phone doing radio shows than I did, I think, with my wife and 2-year-old daughter.

In 1992, I added two more volumes—**"Ace" Any Test** and **Improve Your Memory**, both of which were pretty much written in response to readers' letters. Surprisingly, **Test** and **Memory** quickly became the second- and third-biggest sellers of the seven books in the series, beaten only by **How to Study.** Evidently, my readers knew darned well what they were requesting.

By the way, in both 1992 and 1993, I added mightily to my Frequent Flyer accounts while talking to people nationwide about studying. I wound up visiting 50 cities, some twice, and appearing on more TV and radio shows than are listed in your daily newspaper.

The result of all this travel was twofold: First, sales of all seven books have skyrocketed, in part because of the chance I've been given to talk about them on so many shows and in so many newspapers and magazines. Second, I got to meet and talk with tens of thousands of students and parents, many of whom confirmed the ongoing need for these books *because very little has changed since I first wrote* **How to Study** *some six years ago.*

Test scores of every kind are lower today than they were then. More and more students are dropping out or, if they *do* manage to graduate high school, are finding they are not equipped to do *any*thing, whether they're hoping to go to college or trying to land a job. And more and more parents are frustrated by their children's inability to learn and their schools' seeming inability to teach.

With so much new feedback, it was time to revise all seven books, all of which are being published in time for "back to school" in 1994. In every book, I've included additional topics and expanded on others. I've changed some examples, simplified some, eliminated some. I've rewritten sentences, paragraphs or entire sections that students seemed to be struggling with. Most importantly, I've tried to reflect my new understanding of just who is reading these books—"traditional" students, their parents *and* nontraditional (i.e. older, perhaps much older) students, many of those self-same parents—and write in such a way to include all three audiences.

A couple of caveats

Before we get on with all the tips and techniques you need to take outstanding notes on any topic from any source, let me make two important points about all seven study books.

First, I believe in gender equality, in writing as well as in life. Unfortunately, I find constructions such as "he and she," "s/he," "womyn" and other such stretches to be painfully awkward. I have therefore attempted to sprinkle pronouns of both genders throughout the text. Some teachers, for example, are "he," some are "she." I think this is preferable to using the masculine pronoun throughout but proclaiming one's feminist leanings or to creating so-called "gender-neutral" words or phrases that I find inhibit the "flow" I try to achieve in my writing.

Second, you will find many pieces of advice, examples, lists and other words, phrases and sections spread throughout two or more of the seven books. Certainly *How to Study*, which is an overview of all the study skills, necessarily contains, though in summarized form, some of each of the other six books. But there are discussions of note-taking in *Write Papers* and *Take Notes*, tips about essay tests in *"Ace" Any Test* and *Write Papers*, time management techniques in *Manage Your Time* and *Improve Your Reading*.

The repetition is unavoidable. While I urge everyone to read all seven books in the series, but especially *How to Study*, they *are* seven individual books. And many people only buy one of them. Consequently, I must include in each the pertinent material *for that topic*, even if that material is then repeated in a second or even a third book. As I will point out again and again throughout all the books, these study skills are intimately interrelated. You can't discuss writing papers without covering taking notes for those papers. Or improving your reading without discussing how to take notes from textbooks.

In many cases, not only is the same topic covered, but it is covered in the same language or uses the same example. If I am particularly happy with the way I covered a subject in one book, I have not gone out of my way to completely rewrite a sentence, paragraph or, for that matter, a whole section just to say it "differently" in another. (Besides, for those who follow my advice and work with all seven books, I think the repetition of some of the same important points can only help them learn it more quickly and easily.)

That said, I can guarantee that the nearly 1,000 pages of my *HOW TO STUDY Program* contain the most wide-ranging, comprehensive and complete system of studying ever published. I have attempted to create a system that is useable, that is useful, that is practical, that is learnable. One that *you* can use—whatever your age, whatever your level of achievement, whatever your IQ—to start doing better in school *immediately*.

I hope after reading these books you'll agree I've succeeded.

I'm sure after reading these books that *you'll* succeed.

Ron Fry
May, 1994

THERE *IS* A RIGHT WAY TO TAKE NOTES

Have you or one of your friends ever suffered through an inquisition masquerading as a class? One you slithered into every day with the passion of a eunuch?

Let me tell you about my favorite. It was my friend Tony's eighth-grade American History class with Sister Anne Francis (who did *not* appear in *Forbidden Planet* but probably could have made a convincing Monster of the Id). And it was a note-taking nightmare.

Each day, the good sister filled—twice—all eight black-board panels in the classroom with names, dates, places, wars, rebellions and treaties—more facts than there are people who have seen Madonna's navel. And the students sat there, silently copying *every word* into *their* composition books. No heretical abbreviations or blasphemous shorthand for Sister Anne!

They even had to be careful *how* they copied every word. Their penmanship was expected to be just as perfect as Sister

Anne's; if it wasn't, their grades suffered. (She checked their notebooks once a week!)

They were assigned no reading and no homework. It wasn't until near the end of the semester that Tony found out why: He discovered a textbook ostensibly assigned to the class on a back shelf—which the good sister was merely copying, word for word, every day, onto the blackboard!

That seems like a useless exercise, doesn't it? When all she had to do was just pass out the text?

Unfortunately, the methods most of you are using to take notes are probably not much more useful.

With one difference—here's the book. (Sorry, sister.)

The pitfalls of poor note-taking skills

While most of you will have the good fortune *not* to sit in a classroom commanded by an obsessed nun, too many of you will still develop severe cases of carpel-tunnel syndrome in crazed efforts to reproduce every single word your teachers utter.

Others will take notes so sparse that, when reviewed weeks—or merely hours later—they will make so little sense that they might as well have been etched in Sanskrit.

Taking poor notes—which can mean too *few* or too *many*—will undoubtedly mean poor results. As in, "Here's your D and could you please see me after class?"

If you feel compelled to take down your teacher's every pearly word, or recopy your entire text, you certainly won't have much of a social life—where would you ever find the time? Maybe you're so horrified at the prospect of *reliving* those hours of lectures and chapters of text that you simply *never* review your notes. And if you skip note-taking altogether...well, I don't need to tell you what kind of grades you should expect.

Take Notes

Note-taking should be the ultimate exercise in good old American pragmatism. You should take notes only on the material that helps you develop a thorough understanding of your subject...and get good grades, of course. And you should do it in a way that is, first and foremost, useful and understandable to *you*. A method that's easy to use would be a real plus.

Most students have a difficult time developing a good note-taking technique and recognizing the information that always shows up on tests—an understanding of which is essential for good grades.

Failing to learn good note-taking methods, they resort to what *I* think are useless substitutes, such as tape recorders and photocopying machines.

There is a *right* way to take notes

In this book, I will present the essentials of a note-taking system that works for me and, I'm sure, will work wonders for you. This was not a skill that just came to me, full-blown, like Aphrodite from the ocean, but one that I developed over the years—in high school, college, and on the job as a writer and editor. In the chapters ahead, you will find the distillation of that experience.

And you'll discover that my tried-and-true system is one that is not only easy to learn and *inexpensive,* but one that you can begin using *immediately*—whether taking notes in class, studying a textbook or another reading assignment, gathering information for a term paper or preparing for an exam.

Here's what you'll learn in **Take Notes:** In Chapters 2, 3 and 4 we'll concentrate on what to do *before, during* and *after* class to ensure award-winning class notes. I'll give you my thoughts on tape recorders, discuss the importance of learning to listen, talk about taking notes in different *kinds* of classes, even teach you some shorthand and mapping techniques.

In Chapters 5, 6 and 7, we'll talk about taking notes from your textbooks, covering everything from highlighting and outlining to time lines and concept trees. Plus a new section on working with technical (e.g., math and science) texts.

Chapter 8 introduces my note-taking system for use in the library (the same system used for writing papers). Chapter 9 discusses the slightly different note-taking techniques for preparing an oral vs. a written report. And Chapter 10 gives you a chance to practice all the note-taking skills I'm sure you will have shortly mastered.

Finally, in Chapter 11, I discuss Attention Deficit Disorder (ADD), hyperactivity and the combination condition, ADHD. I have, as a matter of fact, included some version of this chapter in new editions of five of my books (all but *"Ace" Any Test* and *How to Study* itself). While these problems concern a minority of you, it is a large minority and a very concerned one. Parents of children with ADD were usually the first callers on any radio show on which I appeared. Because so many of the study skills I discuss are much more difficult to master for students with ADD, these parents always urged me to address *their* children and point out the tips and techniques *they* needed to learn to succeed in school. With the help of my good friend Thom Hartmann, author of *Attention Deficit Disorder: A Different Perception*, I believe Chapter 11 offers the help these parents asked for.

What's in it for you?

What are the benefits to you when you learn to take better notes? This book will not only help you become better at writing down essential facts, it will help you improve your

Take Notes

listening skills. And guide you toward the path of real learning, rather than just learning how to memorize and repeat names, dates and factoids.

Good note-taking skills will put you in greater control of your time and provide you with a better way to organize your student life. You'll no longer find yourself spending long hours filling notebook after notebook with redundant material, just so you can spend hours rereading it all later. Nor will you ever again need to pull "all-nighters" just before a big test on a subject for which you have inadequate notes.

At test time, you will have the essentials of your class and homework assignments at your fingertips—review will be a breeze.

When you have to research and write a paper, you will have a method that helps you utilize your time in the library and organize the information you gather there more effectively and efficiently. Preparing your reports will be a snap.

But developing your note-taking skills will also benefit you much further down the road. The ability to listen effectively and glean the most salient information from a meeting, speech or presentation will be a required skill in your future—whether you're a doctor making observations for a patient's file, a business executive taking instructions from your CEO for an important project...or a parent jotting down notes as you meet with your child's teacher.

So, take pen in hand, get some paper and start taking better notes...right now.

Chapter One

GATHER YOUR NOTE-TAKING EQUIPMENT

This chapter is short, because my note-taking system is very simple.

There are no expensive kits to send away for.

No special instruments to buy.

No complicated equipment to learn about.

No convoluted instructions you'd need a "techie" to decipher.

Just make sure you have the following materials on hand, and we're ready to go:

1. A ball point pen
2. A three-ring binder with dividers
3. Notebook paper

OK, it's a *little* more complicated—there's one more essential item you need before you can take effective notes:

4. An *active brain*.

Take Notes

Taking notes is a *participatory* activity, whether you're sitting in a lecture or reading a homework assignment. You can't expect to take grade-winning notes if the only thing that's working is your *hand.*

In fact, if you could only bring *one* of the four required items to class, you'd be better off leaving pen, paper and notebook at home.

Ready to go? Do you have everything? Your pen? Paper? Notebook? Brain? Don't worry, I'll show you how to use everything in the following chapters.

Chapter Two

CLASS NOTES: LEARNING TO LISTEN

In one of Bob & Ray's classic radio comedy sketches, Ray plays a talk-show host whose guest is Bob, president of the Slow Talkers of America, which has come to town for its annual convention. The skit goes something like this:

Ray: So, tell me, what brings you to town?

Bob: Well...the...Slow...

Ray: Talkers of America

Bob: Talkers...

Ray: Of America

Bob: Of...

Ray: America

Bob: America...

Take Notes

Ray: Are having their annual convention

Bob: Are...

The impatience of Ray's character is akin to what sometimes happens to *our* minds when we're sitting through a lecture, especially one in which we can find no logical reason to be interested. No matter how fast someone speaks, she cannot deliver information fast enough to keep our minds entirely occupied. The slow pace of orally delivered information is simply not enough to hold our attention.

That's why our thoughts literally go out the window, up to the ceiling, or ahead to Saturday night's date, completely obliterating the lecture from our brain's attention.

This problem is precisely why many businesses are paying big bucks to have their executives take courses on listening. These corporate honchos might be talented, diligent and knowledgeable about their fields, but they are not learning as much as they can from clients and coworkers. Because they never learned how to *listen.*

In fact, many experts in management and education say that listening is one of the most neglected skills in the United States. We assume that if people can *hear,* they can *listen.* But nothing could be further from the truth.

You're probably thinking, "What does all of this have to do with taking notes in class?" The answer: Everything. As I said in the previous chapter, an active brain—one that is prepared to listen and respond—is key to taking effective notes.

I'm convinced that if two students attended a lecture—one copying every word the teacher uttered but not listening to the content; the other listening closely but not taking any notes—the second student would do much better on a surprise quiz at the end of the period.

What makes a good listener *good?*

Have you ever spoken to a good listener? What was it that indicated she was paying attention to you?

- She took her eyes off you only occasionally.
- She wasn't busy formulating a reply as you were speaking.
- She asked frequent questions.

This kind of rapt attention—which you would certainly welcome from anyone sitting through one of *your* stories—is the attitude you should bring to every lecture.

And, believe it or not, note-taking will become a way for you to improve your listening and, of course, remember more of the important information your instructors deliver in class.

"Easier said than done," you sigh? Sure it is. The classroom is as warm as a steambath. The guy in front of you is playing tic-tac-toe on his arm. There's a semi-nude game of frisbee going on just outside the window. And the teacher is delivering a droning soliloquy on the Hottentots' use of damask on castle walls.

Sometimes listening actively is a challenge, if not virtually impossible. But there are steps you can take to make it easier.

Sit near the front of the room

Minimize distractions by sitting as close to the instructor as you can.

Why is it the only time people seem to *want* to be in front is when they're attending a play or a concert? I've noticed that adults who attend meetings, high school or college students in lectures, even churchgoers filling up the pews, inevitably head for the *back* of the room first, as if some deadly disease were lurking on those front-row seats. While this practice gives people at meetings the opportunity to exit unnoticed, it does nothing for students—except make it harder to hear or be heard.

The farther you sit from the teacher, the more difficult it is to listen. Sitting toward the back of the room means more heads bobbing around in front of you, more students staring out the window—encouraging you to do the same.

Sitting up front has several benefits. You will make a terrific first impression on the instructor—you might very well be the only student sitting in the front row. He'll see immediately that you have come to class to listen and learn, not just take up space.

You'll be able to hear the instructor's voice, and the instructor will be able to hear *you* when you ask and answer questions.

Finally, being able to see the teacher clearly will help ensure that your eyes don't wander around the room and out the windows, taking your brain with them.

So, if you have the option of picking your desk in class, sit right down front.

Avoid distracting classmates

The gum cracker. The doodler. The practical joker. The whisperer. Even the perfume sprayer. Your classmates may be wonderful friends, entertaining lunch companions and ultimate weekend party animals, but their quirks, idiosyncrasies and personal hygiene habits can prove distracting when you sit next to them in class.

Knuckle-cracking, giggling, whispering and note-passing are some of the evils that can avert your attention in the middle of your math professor's discourse on quadratic equations. Avoid them.

Sit up straight

To listen effectively, you must sit correctly, in a way that will let you stay comfortable and relatively still during the entire lecture. If you are uncomfortable—if parts of your body start to ache or fall asleep—your attention will inevitably wander from the instructor's words.

As the old saying goes, "The mind can retain only as much as the bottom can sustain."

Listen for verbal clues

Identifying note-worthy material means finding a way to separate the wheat—that which you *should* write down—from the chaff—that which you should *ignore*. How do you do that? By *listening* for verbal clues and *watching* for the nonverbal ones.

Certainly not all teachers will give you the clues you're seeking. But many will invariably signal important material in the way they present it—pausing (waiting for all the pens to rise), repeating the same point (perhaps even one already made and repeated in your textbook), slowing down their normally supersonic lecture speed, speaking more loudly (or more softly), even by simply stating, "I think the following is important."

There are also a number of words that should *signal* note-worthy material (and, at the same time, give you the clues you need to logically organize your notes): "First of all," "Most importantly," "Therefore," "As a result," "To summarize," "On the other hand," "On the contrary," "The following (number of) reasons (causes, effects, decisions, facts, etc.)."

Such words and phrases give you the clues to not just write down the material that follows but to put it in context—to make a list ("First," "The following reasons"); establish a cause-and-effect relationship ("Therefore," "As a result"); establish opposites or alternatives ("On the other hand," "On the contrary"); signify a conclusion ("Therefore," "To summarize"); or offer an explanation or definition.

Look for nonverbal clues

Studies on human behavior indicate that only a small portion of any message is delivered by the words themselves. A greater portion is transmitted by body language, facial expression and tone of voice.

I'll spend some time later in this book helping you learn how to identify the most important points of a lecture, but take advantage of the fact that the instructor—through body language, expressions and tone of voice—will already be doing that identification work for you.

Most instructors will go off on tangents of varying relevance to the subject matter. Some will be important, but, at least during your first few classes with that particular teacher, you won't be able to tell which.

Body language can be your clue.

If the teacher begins looking at the window, or his eyes glaze over, he's sending you a clear signal: "Put your pen down. This isn't going to be on the test. (So don't take notes!)"

On the other hand, if she turns to write something on the blackboard, makes eye contact with several students and/or gestures dramatically, she's sending a clear signal about the importance of the point she's making.

Of course, there are many exceptions to this rule. For example, my first-year calculus instructor would occasionally launch into long diatribes about his mother or air pollution, with tones more impassioned than any he used working through differential equations.

And there was the trigonometry professor I endured who would get most worked up about the damage being done to the nation's sidewalks by the deadly menace of chewing gum.

Nevertheless, learn how to be a detective—don't overlook the clues.

Ask questions often

Being an active listener means asking *yourself* if you understand everything that has been discussed. If the answer is "no," you must ask the instructor questions at an appropriate time or write down the questions you need answered in order to understand the subject fully.

Challenge yourself to draw conclusions from what the instructor is saying. Don't just sit there letting your hand take notes. Let your *mind* do something, too. Think about the subject matter, how it relates to what you've been assigned to read and other facts you've been exposed to.

To tape or not to tape

I am opposed to using a tape recorder in class as a substitute for an active brain for the following reasons:

- *It's time-consuming.* To be cynical about it, not only will you have to waste time sitting in class, you'll have to waste more time listening to that class *again*!

- *It's virtually useless for review.* Fast-forwarding and rewinding cassettes to find the salient points of a lecture is my definition of torture. During the hectic days before an exam, do you really want to waste time listening to a whole lecture when you could just reread your notes, presuming you had some?

Take Notes

- *It offers no back-up.* Only the most diligent students will record *and* take notes. But what happens if your tape recorder malfunctions? How useful will blank or distorted tapes be to you when it's time to review? If you're going to take notes as a back-up, why not just take good notes and leave the tape recorder home?

- *It costs money.* Compare the price of blank paper and a pen to that of recorder, batteries and tapes. The cost of batteries *alone* should convince you that you're better off going the low-tech route.

- When you rely on your tape-recorded lecture for garnering notes, *you miss the "live" clues* we discussed earlier. When all you have is a tape of your lecture, you don't see that zealous flash in your teacher's eyes, the passionate arm-flailing, the stern set of the jaw, any and all of which should scream, "Pay attention. I guarantee this will be on your test!"

Having spent all my fury against tape recorders, I concede that there are times they can be useful. Such as when your head is so stuffed up with a cold that "active listening" during a long lecture is virtually impossible.

Or when the material is so obtuse, you know you have to listen to it more than once just to begin to understand it.

Within the first five minutes of the first lecture of my freshman "honors" physics class at Princeton, I was totally lost—and I knew, even then, I would never *not* be lost. I tried tape recording the class, hoping against hope, I suppose, that listening to the monotone drone of formulas and theorems and hypotheses would somehow make more sense in the quiet of my room than it did in a classful of furiously scratching students.

It didn't help. I understood *less* after listening to the tape. But I'll also admit that it *may* have helped someone less scientifically dense than I.

With these possible exceptions noted, I still maintain that a tape recorder will never be an ample substitute for well-developed listening skills.

(There's one more exception I discuss in more detail in Chapter 11: tape recording as a method for dealing with the poor listening skills associated with ADD.)

Did you get that?

Okay, now that you've learned a little bit about how to listen *actively*, it's time to learn about note-taking strategies. Let's move on to the next chapter.

Chapter Three

CLASS NOTES: SUCCESSFUL STRATEGIES

Note-taking *strategies?*

What could *possibly* be so complicated about taking notes that one would need *strategies.*

After all, it's just a matter of writing down what the instructor says, isn't it? OK, maybe not verbatim, just the key stuff, but...

If you want to take notes *effectively,* there's more to it.

As I've said before, taking down everything the teacher says is *not* an effective strategy. In fact, the most prolific note-takers might be downright *terrible* students.

You can make life easier on yourself if you follow these successful note-taking strategies—and become a *terrific* student in the process.

Know your teacher

First and foremost, you must know and understand the kind of teacher you've got and his or her likes, dislikes, preferences, style and what he or she expects you to get out of the class. Depending on your analysis of your teacher's habits, goals and tendencies, preparation may vary quite a bit, whatever the chosen format.

Take something as simple as asking questions during class, which I encouraged you to do whenever you didn't understand a key point. Some teachers are very confident fielding questions at any time during a lesson; others prefer questions to be held until the end of the day's lesson; still others discourage questions (or any interaction for that matter) entirely. Learn when and how your teacher likes to field questions and ask them accordingly.

No matter how ready a class is to enter into a freewheeling discussion, some teachers fear losing control and veering away from their very specific lesson plan. Such teachers may well encourage discussion but always try to steer it into a predetermined path (their lesson plan). Other teachers thrive on chaos, in which case you can never be sure what's going to happen.

Approaching a class with the former teacher should lead you to participate as much as possible in the class discussion, but warn you to stay within whatever boundaries he or she has obviously set.

Getting ready for a class taught by the latter kind of teacher requires much more than just reading the text—there will be a lot of emphasis on your understanding key concepts, interpretation, analysis and your ability to apply those lessons to cases never mentioned in your text at all!

Some teachers' lesson plans or lectures are, at worst, a review of what's in the text and, at best, a review plus some discussion of sticky points or areas they feel may give you problems. Others use the text or other assignments merely as a jumping-off point—their lectures or lesson plans might cover numerous points that aren't in your text at all. Preparing for the latter kind of class will require much more than rote memorization of facts and figures—you'll have to be ready to give examples, explain concepts in context and more.

Most of your teachers and professors will probably have the same goals: to teach you how to think, learn important facts and principles of the specific subject they teach and, perhaps, how to apply them in your own way.

In classes like math or science, your ability to apply what you've learned to specific problems is paramount.

Others, like your English teacher, will require you to analyze and interpret various works, but may emphasize the "correct" interpretation, too.

Whatever situation you find yourself in—and you may well have one or more of each of the above "types"—you will need to adapt the skills we will cover in this chapter to each situation.

In general, here's how you should plan to prepare for any class before you walk through the door and take your seat:

Complete all assignments

Regardless of a particular teacher's style or the classroom format he or she is using, virtually every course you take will have a formal text (or two or three or more) assigned to it. Though the way the text explains or covers particular topics may differ substantially from your teacher's approach to the same material, your text is still the basis of the course and a key ingredient in your studying. You *must* read it, plus any other assigned books, *before* you get to class.

You may sometimes feel you can get away without reading assigned books beforehand, especially in a lecture format where you *know* the chance of being called on is slim to none. But fear of being questioned on the material is certainly not the only reason I stress reading the material that's been assigned. You will be lost if the professor decides—for the first time ever!—to spend the entire period asking *the students* questions. I've had it happen. And it was *not* a pleasant experience for the unprepared.

You'll also find it harder to take clear and concise notes because you won't know what's in the text (in which case you'll be frantically taking notes on material you could have underlined in your books the night before) or be able to evaluate the relative importance of the teacher's remarks.

If you're heading for a discussion group, how can you participate without your reading as a basis? I think the lousiest feeling in the world is sitting in a classroom knowing that, sooner or later, you are going to be called on...and that you don't know the material at all.

Remember: Completing your reading assignment includes not just reading the *main* text but any *other* books or articles previously assigned, plus handouts that may have been previously passed out. It also means completing any nonreading assignments—turning in a lab report, preparing a list of topics or being ready to present your oral report.

Review your notes

Both from your reading and from the previous class. Your teacher is probably going to start this lecture or discussion from the point he or she left off. You probably won't remember where that point was from week to week...unless you check your notes.

Have questions ready

Go over your questions before class. That way, you'll be able to check off the ones the lecturer or teacher answers along the way and only ask those left unanswered.

Prepare required materials

Including your notebook, text, pens or pencils and other such basics, plus particular class requirements like a calculator, drawing paper or other books.

Before we get into how to take notes, it's important to talk about how to set up your notebook(s). There are a variety of ways you can organize your note-taking system:

1. Get one big two- or three-ring binder (probably three or more inches thick) that will be used for all notes from all classes. This will require a hole punch, "tab" dividers and a healthy supply of pre-punched paper.

   You can divide the binder into separate sections for each course/class, in each of which you will keep notes from your lectures and discussion groups, reading lists, assignment deadlines and any course handouts—all material set up in chronological fashion. Alternatively, you can further subdivide each section into separate sections for reading notes, class notes and handouts.

   The binder offers several advantages over composition books and spiral notebooks:

   - It allows for *easy and neat insertion and removal* of notes. If you've written down a page of notes that you later realize are useless, you can easily get rid of them.

   - More importantly, the binder allows you to *supplement and reorganize* your notes. You can—with the aid of an inexpensive hole puncher—insert hand-outs and pertinent quizzes, photostats of articles from periodicals and completed homework assignments near appropriate notes. Also, if instructors expand upon earlier lessons, you can place your new notes in the right place—they'll make more sense and be more useful when you review for exams and term papers.

- The binder allows you to *travel light*—you don't even have to carry it to class; leave it home. Carry a folder with enough sheets of blank paper to classes; sort your notes and file them in your binder every night. An exercise that will take all of two minutes.

The binder system also has two *dis*advantages:

- Holes that constantly tear, requiring that you patiently paste on those reinforcing circles, a boring and time-wasting task.
- Woe unto ye that lose your binders, for within it is everything ye cherish, and surely ye shall wallow in a sea of incompletes for the rest of your days.

The former problem can be solved by using either a spring-operated binding mechanism—which requires no holes at all, let alone "reinforcements"—or a multi-pocket file folder in which weekly or daily notes can be stapled together and filed along with handouts, assignments, etc.

The latter problem can be solved by selectively "culling" your notebook every week (perhaps at the same time at which you plan the upcoming week?) so, at worst, you lose a week's worth of material, not an entire semester's.

2. Use one of the above systems but get smaller binders, one for each course/class (with the same options regarding the type of binder and how to protect yourself from losing all your notes—if only from a single class).

3. Use separate notebooks (they're a lot lighter than binders) for notes, both from your reading and class. Use file folders for each class to keep handouts, project notes and copies, etc. They can be kept in an accordion file or in a multi-pocketed folder.

Whichever system you choose—one of the above or an ingenious one of your own—do *not* use the note-card system you will learn in Chapter 8. While it's my all-time favorite system for preparing research papers, it does *not* work well for class note-taking...and I've tried it.

Were you listening before?

A young friend of mine boasted that he finished reading the book, *Green Eggs and Ham,* faster than anyone else in his second-grade class. Pleased that he had discovered one of my (and my five-year-old's) favorite Dr. Seuss stories, I asked him what he thought of the book. He replied, "I don't know. I was going so fast, I didn't have time to *read* it."

My friend, bright and eager as he is, had missed the point of his reading assignment. And undoubtedly, had his teacher given a *Green Eggs and Ham* test, he would have scored much lower than some of the slower readers in his class.

If you find yourself furiously filling your notebook pages with your teacher's every pearly word, you might boast the most detailed notes in the class, but I doubt you will truly understand much of what you've so diligently copied.

Why are you taking notes in class?

Are you practicing to enter a speed-writing contest?

Do you want to perfect your dictation-taking skills?

Or are you hoping to actually learn something?

Listen to what your teacher is saying. Think about it. Make sure you understand it. Paraphrase it. *Then,* write your notes.

Learning "selective" listening

Taking concise, clear notes is first and foremost the practice of discrimination—developing your ability to separate the essential from the superfluous, the key concepts, key facts, key ideas from all the rest. In turn, this requires the ability to listen to what your teacher is saying and copying down only what you need to in order to understand the concept. For some, that could mean a single sentence. For others, a detailed example will be the key.

Just remember: The quality of your notes usually has little to do with their *length*—three key lines that reveal the core concepts of a whole lecture are far more valuable than paragraphs of less important data.

So why do some people keep trying to take verbatim notes, convinced that the more pages they cover with scribbles the better students they're being? It's probably a sign of insecurity—they haven't read the material and/or don't have a clue about what's being discussed, but at least they'll have complete notes!

Even if you find yourself wandering helplessly in the lecturer's wake, so unsure of what she's saying that you can't begin to separate the important, note-worthy material from the nonessential verbiage, use the techniques discussed in this book to organize and condense your notes anyway.

If you really find yourself so lost that you are just wasting your time, consider adding a review session to your schedule (to read or reread the appropriate texts) and, if the lecture or class is available again at another time, attend again. Yes, it *is*, strictly speaking, a waste of your precious study time, but *not* if it's the only way to learn and understand important material.

Understand the big picture

If you are actively listening, and listening before you write, then your understanding of the "big picture" (with apologies to A. Whitney Brown) ought to follow naturally.

Let's say your history teacher is rattling off dates and names of battles from the Franco-Prussian War. Your classmates in the back of the room may go into a panic as they scramble to jot down all the tongue-twisting foreign names that are being spewed out at machine-gun speed.

But *you*, who are sitting up front and listening actively, pause, pen in hand, as your teacher sums up her point: that battle activity increased to a frenzy in the final months before war's end. You jot down a brief note to that effect, knowing that you can check your textbook later for all the names, dates and details of specific battles.

Your poor friends in the back, while capturing most of the battle names, missed the main point—the big picture—and now will feel compelled to memorize the list of names and dates, even though they can't quite figure out why they copied them down in the first place.

Take notes on what you *don't* know

You *know* the first line of the Gettysburg address. You *know* the chemical formula for water. You *know* what date Pearl Harbor was bombed. So why waste time and space writing them down?

Frequently, your teachers will present material you already know in order to set the stage for further discussion, or to introduce material that is more difficult. Don't be so conditioned to automatically copy down dates, vocabulary, terms, formulas and names that you mindlessly take notes on information you already know. You'll just be wasting your time—both in class and, later, when you review your overly detailed notes.

Tailor your note-taking to class format

The extent of note-taking required—as well as the importance of those notes to your success in class—will depend to a great extent on the format of each class. There are three different types you'll need to know and adapt to:

- *The lecture.* Teacher speaks, you listen. While some high-school teachers conduct classes in this relatively impersonal way, this format is usually adapted for popular college courses, such as Geology 101 (*aka* "Rocks for Jocks"). In such situations, your teacher might never even know your name. Consequently, your note-taking and listening skills are the only tools you'll be able to use in your quest for top grades.
- *The seminar.* Again, more common at the college level, seminars are also known as *tutorials* or *discussion groups.* Usually conducted by graduate students, they are often held in conjunction with the larger lectures, giving students a chance to discuss the subject matter in a group of less than a hundred.

  While this format places a great deal of emphasis on your question-asking and answering skills, you should not neglect your note-taking skills. Be all ears while the discussion is flowing, but, as soon as possible *after* class, write down the most important points discussed. (Most high school classes are a combination of a lecture—the teacher introducing the particular material in that day's lesson plan—and a discussion group, which may just as often be a question-

and-answer session, with the teacher doing the questioning.)

- ***Hands-on classes.*** Science and language labs, art classes and courses in industrial arts will require you to *do* something. But *while* you are doing it, remember to keep a notebook handy.

    I had a chemistry teacher who, during labs, quite often launched into extensive theoretical discussions. The less dull-witted among us quickly learned to keep our notebooks close by, capturing facts and figures he never mentioned again—except on the exams!

Observe your instructor's style

All instructors (perhaps I should say all *effective* instructors) develop a plan of attack for each class. They decide what points they will make, how much time they will spend reviewing assignments and previous lessons, what texts they will refer to, what anecdotes they will bring into the lecture to provide comic relief or human interest, how much time they'll allow for questions.

Building a note-taking strategy around each instructor's typical plan of attack for lectures is another key to academic success.

Throughout junior high school and much of high school, I had to struggle to get good grades. I took copious notes, studied them every night, pored over them before every quiz and exam.

I was rewarded for my efforts with straight As, but resented the hours I had to put in while my less ambitious buddies found more intriguing ways to spend their time.

But some of the brighter kids had leisure time, too. When I asked them how they did it, they shrugged their shoulders and said they didn't know.

These students had an innate talent that they couldn't explain, a sixth sense about what to study, what were the most important things a teacher said, what instructors were most likely to ask about on tests.

In fact, when I was in a study group with some of these students, they would say, "Don't worry, she'll never ask about that." And sure enough, she never did.

What's more, these students had forgotten many of the details I was sweating. They hadn't even bothered to write any of them down, let alone try to remember them.

What these students innately knew was that items discussed during any lesson could be grouped into several categories, which varied in importance:

- Information not contained in the class texts and other assigned readings
- Explanations of obscure material covered in the texts and readings but with which students might have difficulty
- Demonstrations or examples that provided greater understanding of the subject matter
- Background information that put the course material in context

As you are listening to an instructor, decide which of these categories best fits the information being presented. This will help you determine how detailed your notes on the material should be. (This will become especially easy as you get to know the instructor.)

An example that comes to mind is that of a physics professor I had who devoted about half of every session to an examination of an important mathematician's or physicist's life and the circumstances surrounding his or her discoveries. At first, I took copious notes on these lectures, only to find that the first two exams were filled, top to bottom, with problems and formulae, not biographical questions.

Needless to say, even *I* figured out that I shouldn't take such comprehensive notes about biographical details.

Read, read, read

Most good instructors will follow a text they've selected for the course. Likewise, unless they've written the textbook themselves (which you will find surprisingly common in college), most teachers will supplement it with additional information. Good teachers will look for shortcomings in textbooks and spend varying amounts of class time filling in these gaps.

As a result, it makes sense to stay one step ahead of your instructors. Read ahead in your textbook so that, as an instructor is speaking, you know what part of the lesson you should write down and what parts of it are *already* written down in your textbook. Conversely, you'll immediately recognize the supplemental material on which you might need to take more detailed notes.

Will you be asked about this supplemental material on your exams?

Of course, if you ask your teacher that question, he'll probably say something like, "You are expected to know everything that's mentioned in this class." That's why it's best to pay attention (and not ask stupid questions you already know the answers to!).

You'll quickly learn to tell from a teacher's body language what he or she considers important and what's tangential. (See Chapter 2 for more on this.)

In addition, your experience with the teacher's exams and spot quizzes will give you a great deal of insight into what he or she considers most important.

Instant replay: Review your notes

My friend Tony worked for a time as a reporter on a trade magazine. He would take voluminous notes as sources were talking to him. Days later, as he reread these notes, he'd invariably discover that he really didn't have any full, direct quotes—just snatches of sentences. He couldn't write fast enough to capture the whole thing.

The solution? No, it *wasn't* a tape recorder. It was to read the notes over *immediately* after the conversation. This would allow him to fill in the blanks, putting in the words he couldn't take down at conversational speed.

You should do the same with your class notes. Take the time to look them over briefly at lunch breaks, in study halls, when you go home. Honestly evaluate whether they will be decipherable when it comes time to study for your exams. If not, add to them what you can *while your memory of the class is still fresh.*

Even as you implement these strategies, which will reduce the amount of time you're scribbling notes, you'll still find yourself in situations where you want to capture a lot of information—quickly.

I'll show you how in the next chapter.

Chapter Four

MAKING SHORT WORK OF CLASS NOTES

You don't have to be a master of shorthand to streamline your note-taking. Here are five ways:

1. *Eliminate vowels.* As a sign that was ubiquitous in the New York City subways used to proclaim, "If u cn rd ths, u cn gt a gd jb." (If you can read this, you can get a good job.) And, we might add, "u cn b a btr stdnt."

2. *Use word beginnings* ("rep" for representative, "con" for congressperson) and other easy-to-remember abbreviations.

3. *Stop putting periods* after all abbreviations (they add up!)

4. *Use standard symbols* in place of words. Here is a list that will help you out in most of your classes (you may recognize many of these symbols from math and logic):

≈	*Approximately*
w/	*With*
w/o	*Without*
wh/	*Which*
→	*Resulting in*
←	*As a result of/consequence of*
+	*And or also*
*	*Most importantly*
cf	*Compare; in comparison; in relation to*
ff	*Following*
<	*Less than*
>	*More than*
=	*The same as, equal to*
↑	*Increasing*
↓	*Decreasing*
esp	*Especially*
Δ	*Change*
⊂	*It follows that*
∴	*Therefore*
∵	*Because*

5. ***Create your own symbols*** and abbreviations based on your needs and comfort-level.

There are two specific symbols I think you'll want to create—they'll be needed again and again:

Ⓦ That's my symbol for "*What?*", as in "What the heck does that mean", "What did she say?" or "What happened? I'm completely lost!" It denotes *something* that's been missed—leave space in your notes to fill in the missing part of the puzzle after class.

(M) That's my symbol for "My idea" or "My thought." I want to clearly separate my own thoughts during a lecture from the professor's—put in too many of your own ideas (without noting that they *are* yours) and your notes begin to lose some serious value!

Feel free to use your own code for these two important instances; you certainly don't have to use mine.

While I recommend using all the "common" symbols and abbreviations listed previously *all* the time, in *every* class, in order to maintain consistency, you may want to create specific symbols or abbreviations for each class. In chemistry, for example, "TD" may stand for thermodynamics, "K" for the Kinetic Theory of Gases (but don't mix it up with the "K" for Kelvin). In history, "GW" is the Father of our country, "ABE" is Mr. Honesty, "FR" could be French Revolution (or "freedom rider"), "IR", the Industrial Revolution.

How do you keep everything straight? No matter what, summarize your abbreviations on each class's notes, perhaps on the front page in a corner. If you're a little more adventurous, create a list on the first page of that class's notebook or binder section for the abbreviations and symbols you intend to use regularly through the semester.

Expanding on your 'shorthand'

While you're listening to your instructor, you should be thinking about what you write down. Lectures are filled with so many words that will not be at all helpful when you sit down to study for the big exam. Writing all of *those* words down—while missing some of the truly important points of the lecture—is counterproductive: Your notes may look impressively complete, but what are they completely full *of?* All the important stuff, or...?

For instance, if your teacher says, "It's surprising to me that so few people know the role that women pilots played in World War II. We normally hear only about 'Rosie the Riveter' and the role women played at *home*. But the shortage of male pilots at the beginning of the war virtually demanded that women be given a chance, if only, in some areas, to ferry planes, tow targets or test repaired planes." you could write down something like:

> Wmn's rl/PLs—WW2 <'
> short/men: Ferry Ps/tow tgts/test
> rep Ps

I've written "PL" for pilot and "P" for plane presuming that both words will occur frequently in a lecture on this topic. The more frequently a term occurs, the *more* reason you have to simplify it, preferably to a single letter. But I wrote out "ferry," a word that would not tend to come up too often, as well as "test," figuring the extra "e" in both wouldn't take much time.

Continue to abbreviate *more* as additional terms become readily recognizable—in that way, the speed and effectiveness of your note-taking will increase as the school year grinds on.

I've also noticed that many students are prone to write *big* when they are writing fast and to use only a portion of the width of their paper. I guess they figure that turning over pages quickly means they are taking great notes. All it really means is that they are taking notes that will be difficult to read or use when it's review time.

Force yourself to write small and take advantage of the entire width of your note paper. The less unnecessary movement the better.

In this and the preceding chapter, I've discussed how to prepare and implement a note-taking strategy in class. Now,

Take Notes

let's look at a sample lecture so you can practice your newly developed skills.

Here is part of a lecture that was one of my favorites in college. I've numbered the paragraphs here so that they can be referred to easily later.

The Comic Perspective In Comic Novels

1 The comic perspective is one which finds its most successful expression in a presentation of contrasting methods of viewing the world. These could be categorized as that of the cynic and that of the saint. The laughter and the sense of irony that a comic work of literature can instill in its readers is a result of the clash between these methods of seeing the world.

2 If the work of literature is to be considered at all successful, its readers will surely find themselves beset with the task of sorting among the alternatives offered by the idealistic and realistic sensibilities embodied within the characters and/or the narrative voice.

3 The comic novel is one which, at last, must leave its readers experiencing its world in the way a child experiences his; with wonder, honesty, imagination and confusion.

4 If we conduct an overview of protagonists in great comic novels, we find characters who are very much like children. They are innocent, idealistic and often naive. Moreover, authors of the great comic novels go to great lengths to deny their characters a detailed past. It is almost as if the protagonists are born fully grown into the world of the novel.

5 We can learn very few biographical details about Don Quixote. We are told only that he has filled his head

with the ideals and dreams of chivalry through his incessant reading of romantic literature. Moving ahead to Dickens, we find in <u>The Pickwick Papers</u> a protagonist that the author continually denies a past. It is as if, for Dickens, the intrusion or even the introduction of the past into the present must inevitably bring with it a diminution of integrity and self-sufficiency. In fact, the only instance of Mr. Pickwick attempting to remember his past results in the protagonist falling asleep before he can do so.

6 When we get to the 20th-century comic novels we notice a continuity of this device. Paul Pennyfeather is delivered into the chaotic world of <u>Decline and Fall</u> as if from a womb. Evelyn Waugh devotes three sentences to the history of his protagonist. He is an orphan (someone who by definition cannot know his past) who "lived in Onslow Square with his guardian, who was abysmally bored by his company..."

While you don't have the luxury of being able to *hear* these words, as, of course, you would in a real lecture, pretend that you were suddenly stripped of the benefits afforded by the printed page—the ability to reread a portion of a lecture that you wouldn't be able to "rehear."

What would you come up with? How many of the actual words from the lecture would turn up in your notes? Would you be trying to get down everything the professor said?

While this lecture *sounds* eloquent, it has more sizzle to it than steak. Hence, your notes can be quite brief. Here are what mine looked like (with the paragraph references added):

Cmc Prspctv/Cmc Nvls

1. CP=2 wys 2 C wrld—cynic, saint. Clash=lftr
2. Chrctrs, nrrtr embdy idlsm or rlsm

3. Rdr xprnc=chld's wrld view=cnfused, inncnt
4. Prtgnsts like kids—no past
5. eg Dk/PP, Cv/DQ
6. eg EW/Pnnyf

Lincoln in shorthand

I readily admit that reducing an instructor's eloquent words to this type of shorthand is like summarizing Lincoln's "Gettysburg Address" as:

> "Bad war. Guys died. What a shame. Hope it
> ends soon."

Trying to capture the eloquence and missing half of the teacher's points would make much less sense. And note that very little effort has been put into this "shorthand" approach—a few symbols (=, eg), a couple of obvious substitutions (2 for two, C for see) and the omission of most vowels. Yet it is organized, understandable and took a minimum of time to write down.

What taking such brief notes will do is allow you to sit back, listen and watch the instructor. This will help you capture the entire *message* that he or she is communicating, not just the *words*. If you think that the words are very important, try to elaborate on your shorthand while the professor's words are still rattling around in your head—right after the lecture. It's not a bad idea to do this anyway, especially as you start to develop your own note-taking shorthand. It'll allow you to make sure you understand your own abbreviations.

Are you ready to lose the vowels

Do you think this sort of shorthand will work for you? You probably won't at first. When I first entered college, I found that I couldn't trust my notes. I was trying to write too much down, which meant that I couldn't trust my note-*taking*. As I gained more experience and developed much of the system in this and the previous two chapters, my note-taking became more and more productive.

Just be careful—in your fervor to adopt my shorthand system, don't abbreviate so much that your notes are absolutely unintelligible to you almost as soon as you write them!

Just come up with a note-taking shorthand system that makes sense to *you*. You may certainly choose to abbreviate less, to write a little more. Whatever system you develop, make sure it serves the right purpose: giving you the time to really *listen* to your instructors, rather than writing down only what they say.

Draw your way to good grades

The one problem with this whole note-taking system I've discussed is that many people find it more difficult to remember words rather than pictures.

Problem solved: *Mapping* is another way to take notes that stresses a more visual style—drawing or diagramming your notes rather than just writing them down.

Let me show you how to map the first few pages of this chapter as an example. Start with a clean sheet of paper and, boxed or circled in the center, write the main topic:

Developing shorthand skills

How do you want your picture to read—top to bottom, bottom to top, clockwise in a circle, counterclockwise? I'm going to set mine up clockwise, starting at the top (12 o'clock). After deciding on the first major topic ("How to streamline note-taking") and placing it on your map, add the detail:

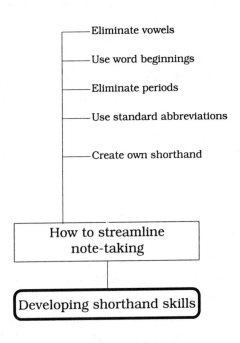

The second major topic ("Expanding your shorthand") and those that follow take their place in the circle you've chosen in the direction you've chosen. I've completed a map containing everything covering up to our discussion of mapping on page 54.

Talk the talk

In many nonlecture classes, you will find that discussion, mostly in the form of questions and answers, is actively encouraged. This dialogue serves to both confirm your knowledge and comprehension of specific subject matter and identify those areas in which you need work.

Whatever the format in which you find yourself, participate in any discussion to the best of your ability. Most teachers consider class participation a key ingredient in the grades they mete out. No matter how many papers and tests you ace, if you never open your mouth in class, you may be surprised (but shouldn't be) to get less than an A.

If you are having trouble following a particular line of thought or argument, ask for a review or for clarification.

Don't ask questions or make points looking to impress your teacher—your real motive will probably be pretty obvious. Remember what you *are* there for—to learn the material and master it.

Based on the professor's preferences and the class set-up, ask the questions you feel need answers.

Be careful you don't innocently distract yourself from practicing your now-excellent note-taking skills by either starting to analyze something you don't understand or, worse, creating mental arguments because you disagree with something your teacher or a classmate said. Taking the time to mentally frame an elaborate question is equally distracting. All three cause the same problem: *You're not listening!*

Finally, listen closely to the words of your classmates. Knowledge has no boundaries, and you'll often find their comments, attitudes and opinions as helpful and insightful as your instructor's.

What if you're shy or just get numb whenever you're called on? Ask a question rather than taking part in the discussion— it's easier and, over time, may help you break the ice and jump into the discussion. If you really can't open your mouth without running a fever, consider a remedial course, like Dale Carnegie.

Take Notes

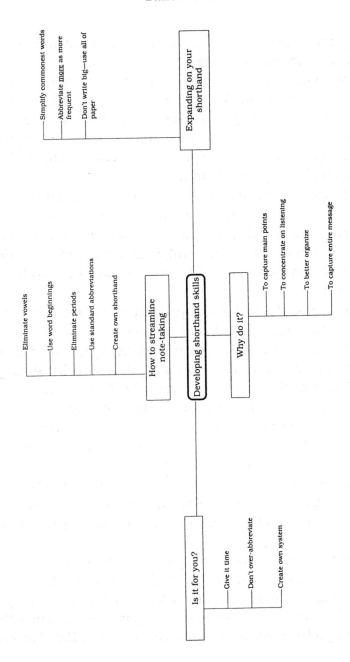

Developing shorthand skills

Expanding on your shorthand
- Simplify commonest words
- Abbreviate _more_ as more frequent
- Don't write big—use all of paper

How to streamline note-taking
- Eliminate vowels
- Use word beginnings
- Eliminate periods
- Use standard abbreviations
- Create own shorthand

Why do it?
- To capture main points
- To concentrate on listening
- To better organize
- To capture entire message

Is it for you?
- Give it time
- Don't over-abbreviate
- Create own system

Most importantly, prepare and practice. Fear of standing in front of a class or even of participating from the safety of your seat is, for many of you, really a symptom of lack of confidence.

And *lack of confidence stems from lack of preparation.* The more prepared you are—if you know the material backwards and forwards—the more likely you will be able, even *want,* to raise your hand and "strut your stuff." Practicing with friends, parents or relatives may also help.

If you are having trouble with oral reports, they are covered separately in Chapter 9. I think you'll find the hints I've included there will eliminate a lot of the fear such talks seem to engender.

What to do *after* class

As soon as possible after your class, review your notes, fill in the "blanks," mark down questions you need to research in your text or ask during the next class, and remember to mark any new assignments on your weekly calendar.

I tend to discourage recopying your notes as a general practice, since I believe it's more important to work on taking good notes the first time around. *But* if you tend to write fast and illegibly, it might also be a good time to rewrite your notes so they're readable, taking the opportunity to summarize as you go. The better your notes, the better your chance of capturing and recalling the pertinent material.

It is not easy for most high school students to do so, but in college, where you have a greater say in scheduling your classes, this is why I recommend "one period on, one off"—an open period, even a half hour, after each class to review that class's notes and prepare for the next one.

Since I stressed so often the importance of reading your texts *before* you stroll into the classroom, let's turn our attention to what you need to do *out*side of class in order to be a star *in* class.

Chapter Five

TEXTS: READ FIRST, THEN WRITE

I'm sure it's abundantly clear to all of you that not many best-selling authors moonlight writing textbooks. Most of the tomes given to you in classes—even the ones for *literature* classes—are poorly written, badly organized cures for insomnia. Dull is the kindest word to describe all but a few of them.

That said, it's also clear that no matter how dull the prose, your job is to mine the important details from your textbooks to get good grades. Lest you have to wade through that lifeless mass of words more than once, why not take great notes the *first* time through?

You can borrow many of the strategies you implemented for taking notes in class for your attack on your reading assignments. Just as you used your active brain to listen carefully to what your teacher talked about, you can use that same piece of equipment to *read* actively.

Read, then write.

Make sure you understand the big picture.

Take notes on what you don't know.

These same principles we discussed in conjunction with taking notes in class apply to taking notes on your reading materials. But there are some additional strategies you should also consider.

Change the way you read

When we read a book for pleasure, we tend to read, naturally, from beginning to the end. (Though some of us may be guilty of taking a peek at the last chapter of a suspenseful mystery novel.) Yet this linear approach, beginning at point A and moving in a direct manner to point B, is not necessarily the most effective way to read texts for information.

If you find yourself plowing diligently through your texts without having the faintest clue as to what you've read, it's time to change the way you read. The best students don't wade through each chapter of their textbooks from beginning to end. Instead, they read in an almost circular fashion. Here's how:

Look for clues

If we have curled up with the latest Stephen King thriller, we fully expect some clues along the way that will hint at the gory horror to come. And we count on Agatha Christie to subtly sprinkle keys to her mysteries' solutions long before they are resolved in the drawing room.

But most of you probably never tried to solve the mystery of your own textbooks by using the telltale signs and signals almost all of them contain. That's right—*textbooks are riddled with clues* that will reveal to the perceptive student all the note-worthy material that must be captured. Here's where to find them:

Chapter heads and subheads. Bold-faced headings and subheadings announce the detail about the main topic. And, in some textbooks, paragraph headings or bold-faced "lead-ins" announce that the author is about to provide finer details. So start each reading assignment by going through the chapter, beginning to end, but *reading only the bold-faced heads and subheads.*

This process of headline reading takes only a few minutes, but it lays the groundwork for a more intelligent and efficient reading of the chapter. You'll have some idea where the author is headed, and this will give you a greater sense of what the most important details are.

End-of-chapter summaries. If you read a mystery from start to finish, the way the author hopes you will, you're likely to get thrown off the scent of the murderer by "red herrings" and other common detective novel devices. However, if you read the last part first, knowing the outcome would help you notice how the author constructed the novel and built an open-and-shut case for his master sleuth. You'd notice a plethora of details about the eventually unmasked murderer that might have gone unnoticed were she just another of the leading suspects.

Similarly, knowing what the author is driving at in a textbook will help you look for the important building blocks for his conclusions while you're reading. While it may not be as much fun to read a mystery novel this way, when it comes to textbook reading and note-taking, it will make you a much more *active* reader, and, consequently, make it much less likely that you will doze off while being beaten senseless by the usual ponderous prose.

Pictures, graphs, charts. Most textbooks, particularly those in the sciences, will have charts, graphs, numerical tables, maps and other illustrations. All too many students see these as mere filler—padding to glance at, then forget.

If you're giving these charts and graphs short shrift, you're really shortchanging *yourself.* You don't have to redraw the tables in your notes, but it would be helpful to observe how they supplement the text, what points they emphasize and make note of these. This will help you put them into your own words, which will help you remember them later. And it will ensure that you don't have to continually refer to your textbooks when brushing up for an exam.

Highlighted terms, vocabulary and other facts. In some textbooks, you'll discover that key terms and information are highlighted within the body text. (And I *don't* mean by a previous student; consider such yellow-swathed passages with caution—their value is directly proportional to that student's final grade, which you don't know.) Whether bold-face, italic or boxed, this is usually an indication that the material is noteworthy.

Questions. Some textbook publishers use a format in which key points are emphasized by questions, either within the body or at the end of the chapter. If you read these questions *before* reading the chapter, you'll have a better idea of what material you need to pay closer attention to.

These standard organizational tools should make your reading job simpler. The next time you have to read a history, geography or similar text, try skimming the assigned pages first.

Read the heads, the subheads and the call outs. Read the first sentence of each paragraph. Then go back and start reading the details.

To summarize the skimming process:

1. Read and be sure you understand the title or heading. Try rephrasing it as a question for further clarification of what you will read.
2. Examine all the subheadings, illustrations and graphics—these will help you identify the significant matter within the text.
3. Read *thoroughly* the introductory paragraphs, the summary at the end and any questions at chapter's end.
4. Read the first sentence of every paragraph—this generally includes the main idea.
5. Evaluate what you have gained from this process: Can you answer the questions at the end of the chapter? Could you intelligently participate in a class discussion of the material?
6. Write a brief summary that capsulizes what you have learned from your skimming.
7. Based on this evaluation, decide whether a more thorough reading is required.

Now for the fine print

Now that you have gotten a good overview of the contents by reading the heads and subheads, reviewing the summary, picking up on the highlighted words and information and considering the review questions that may be included, you're finally ready to read the chapter.

If a more thorough reading is then required, turn back to the beginning. ***Read one section (chapter, etc.) at a time.*** And do not go on to the next until you've completed the following exercise:

1. Write definitions of any key terms you feel are essential to understanding the topic.
2. Write questions and answers you feel clarify the topic.
3. Write any questions for which you *don't* have answers—then make sure you find them through re-reading, further research or asking another student or your teacher.
4. Even if you still have unanswered questions, move on to the next section and complete numbers 1 to 3 for that section. (And so on, until your reading assignment is complete.)

See if this method doesn't help you get a better handle on any assignment right from the start.

Because you did a preliminary review first, you'll find that your reading will go much faster.

But...don't assume that now you can speed through your reading assignment. Don't rush through your textbook, or you'll just have to read it again.

Sure, we've all heard about the boy and girl wonders who can whip through 1,000 or even 2,000 words per minute and retain it all, but most of us never will read that fast. Which is fine—it's better to read something slowly and *remember* it, than rush it into oblivion.

Many great students—even those in law school or taking umpteen courses on the 19th-century novel—never achieve reading speeds of even close to 1,000 words per minute. Some of them have to read passages they don't understand again and again to get the point.

And there's nothing wrong with that.

This is the most intelligent way to read—with *comprehension*, not speed—as your primary goal.

Reading technical texts

Math and science texts (or any highly technical ones, like economics) require slightly different handling. Do everything covered in our discussion of skimming texts, with one addition: Make *sure* you understand the concepts expressed in the various graphs or charts.

But do *not proceed* to the next chapter or even the next section if you have questions about the previous one. You must understand one section before moving on to the next, since the next concept is usually based on the previous one. If there are sample problems, solve those that tie in with the section you have just read to make sure you understand the concepts imparted. If you still fail to grasp a key concept, equation, etc., start again and try again. But *don't* move on—you'll just be wasting your time.

These texts really require such a slow, steady approach, even one with a lot of backtracking or, for that matter, a lot of wrong turns. "Trial and error" *is* an accepted method of scientific research. The key, though, is to make it *informed* trial and error—having a clear idea of where you're heading and *learning* from each error. While trial and error is okay, it is much more important to be able to easily apply the same analysis (solution, reasoning) to a slightly different problem, which requires real understanding. Getting the right answer just because you eliminated every *wrong* one may be a very viable strategy for taking a test but it's a lousy way to assure yourself you've actually learned something.

Understanding is especially essential in any technical subjects. Yes, it's easy for some of you to do great on math tests because you have a great memory and/or are lucky and/or have an innate math "sense." Trust me, sooner or later, your luck runs out, your memory overloads and your calculations become "sense"-less. You *will* reach a point where, without understanding, you will be left confused on the shore, watching your colleagues stroke heroically off to the promised land.

It happened to me in college, where I was (*very* briefly) an electrical engineering major. As long as logarithms and integral calculus were theoretical—just remember the rules, get a little lucky and count on my built-in math "radar"—I could shine. Not only did I get a perfect 800 on the math section of the SAT, I got an 800 on the *Calculus Achievement Test* (now the SAT-II). A budding mathematical genius, *ne c'est pas?*

Sure. Until I had to actually show I *understood* the concepts underlying all the rules and calculations, to use that understanding as the basis for practical reasoning and applying the concepts. Remember the TV show *Lost in Space*? Me during freshman year physics *and* physical chemistry. Good-by "math sense", hello English major.

Whether math and science come easily to you or make you want to find the nearest pencil-pocketed computer nerd and throttle him, there are some ways you can do better at such technical subjects, without the world's greatest memory, a lot of luck or any "radar":

- Whenever you can, "translate" formulas and numbers into words. To test your understanding, try to put your translation into *different* words.

Take Notes

- Even if you're not particularly visual, pictures can often help. Try translating a particularly vexing math problem into a drawing or diagram.
- Before you even get down to solving a problem, is there any way for you to estimate the answer or, at least, to estimate the range within which the answer should fall (greater than 1, but less than 10)? This is the easy way to at least make sure you wind up in the right ballpark.
- Play around. There are often different paths to the same solution, or even equally valid solutions. If you find one, try to find others. This is a great way to increase your understanding of all the principles involved.
- When you are checking your calculations, try working *back*wards. I've found it an easier way to catch simple arithmetical errors.
- Try to figure out what is being asked, what principles are involved, what information is important, what's not. (I can't resist an example here, one that was thrown at me in 8th grade: Picture a record—the vinyl kind, before CDs. Its diameter is 9 inches. The label is perfectly centered. Its radius is 1.75 inches. The record plays at 45 revolutions per minute, and the song it plays lasts for exactly 3 minutes. The vinyl is exactly .18 mm thick.

    Got it? OK, here's the question: How many grooves does the record have?)
- Teach someone else. Trying to explain mathematical concepts to someone else will quickly pinpoint what you really know or don't know. It's virtually impossible to get someone else—especially someone

who is slower than you at all this stuff—to understand if you don't!

(By the way, the answer is "one." Any *more* than one continuous groove and the song wouldn't keep playing. In case you didn't notice, *none* of the mathematical information given had the slightest bearing on the answer.)

Reading foreign language texts

Foreign language texts should be approached the same way, especially basic ones teaching vocabulary. If you haven't mastered the words you're supposed to in the first section, you'll have trouble reading the story at the end of section three, even if you've learned all the words in sections two and three. So take it one step at a time and make sure you have mastered one concept, vocabulary list, lesson, etc., before jumping ahead.

For a further exploration of how to read for class more effectively, I suggest you pick up a copy of the brand-new second edition of *Improve Your Reading,* another of the seven volumes in my **HOW TO STUDY** *Program.*

Chapter Six

TEXTS: NOW GET OUT YOUR PEN

Mr. Lonney's assignment sounded simple enough: Read the photocopy of the *The Atlantic* magazine article about Hemingway's years in Key West for a quiz on Friday. A fairly typical assignment that three students in the class chose to tackle in three completely different ways:

Sally read the article with her legs over the side of a sofa during a "Star Trek" rerun. In this way, she missed most of the salient points in the article, though not what the trouble with tribbles really was (for the thirteenth time). During commercials, however, she really hunkered down and paid close attention to what she was reading. This made Sally quite proud of herself—she usually didn't bother to read assignments at all, particularly ones as boring as this one.

Kevin spent an hour at his desk on Thursday night reading the article—twice—and highlighting what he felt were the most important parts. He was confident that he had a good grasp of the material and completely understood the most important points of the article.

Barb spent about three hours going back and forth between the article and a legal pad, writing down long, complete sentences that, all told, summarized the salient points and a good many details of the article pretty well. She planned to read over the notes during the study hall she had before Mr. Lonney's class.

Who got the best grade?

Barb put in the most time. And she did get an A. Kevin earned a B+. Sally was pretty happy with the C- she didn't have to work too hard for.

Who had the right approach? Barb, right?

Wrong. The answer is that old favorite of the multiple-choice test: none of the above.

"A" is *not* for effort

Even though the ends in some way justified Barb's means, the amount of effort she puts into most of her assignments also ensures that she doesn't have much of a personal life. She regularly works until 11 p.m., and puts in quite a few hours cracking the books on weekends.

Admirable?

Or overkill?

Well, then, you're thinking, why doesn't Kevin have the right idea? After all, he put in only an hour and got a grade pretty darn close to Barb's.

Actually, if Kevin had spent the *same* amount of time—but used it more wisely—he could have turned that B+ into an A...with*out* working *harder*.

Work smarter, not harder

The right approach to Mr. Lonney's assignment lies somewhere between Kevin's and Barb's. (Sorry, Sally.) Careful reading and good notes are essential to earning good grades consistently. But taking good notes on written materials does not have to take a lot of time. With a good note-taking system, Barb could have gotten to bed an hour earlier (or caught that "Star Trek" rerun herself).

Effective note-taking skills should:

- **Help you recognize** the most important points of a text
- **Make it easier** for you to understand those important points
- **Enhance your memory** of the text
- Provide a **highly efficient** way to study for your exams

Let's learn how to take better notes on this sort of material and practice doing it.

Go for the gold, ignore the pyrite

Step one in effective note taking from texts is to write down the *principle* points the author is trying to make. These main ideas should be placed either in the left-hand margin of your note paper, or as headings. *Do not write complete sentences.*

Then, write down the most important details or examples the author uses to support each of these arguments. These details should be noted under their appropriate main idea. I suggest indenting them and writing each idea on a new line, one under the other. Again, *do not use complete sentences.* Include only enough details so that your notes are not "Greek to you" when you review them.

A note-taking exercise

Let's practice these steps using the following article.

The Effects of Mabel Dodge Luhan on the Cultural and Social Life of Taos, New Mexico

Mabel Dodge Luhan had an extraordinary effect on the life of the little mountain town of Taos, New Mexico. From the time she arrived in 1917 until her death in 1962, Mabel was the social and cultural life of the town. She not only brought her own personality to the artists' colony, but numerous artists and writers to visit Taos as well. Some of them remained in the area for the rest of their lives.

The gatherings of these famous people—D.H. Lawrence, Georgia O'Keeffe, Greta Garbo, Leopold Stokowski and others—in Mabel's house served as a kind of "salon" where important members of the American and European artistic communities met, discussed each other's work, and spread the word about Taos and Mabel when they returned to New York, California or Europe. Their enthusiasm helped bring even more famous people to visit Taos.

The social scene in Taos centered on Mabel. Because she was a personal friend of most of the people who visited her, as well as being wealthy, domineering and extremely active, she reigned as the head of the social order in the town during her entire lifetime. The other prominent members of the community—the artists, the wealthy ranchers, the merchants—all formed a pecking order beneath her.

Mabel's support of the artistic community earlier in this century helped spread the fame of these artists—and in-

Take Notes

creased the sale of their works. The prominence of Taos as an artists' colony, thanks in part to Mabel, encouraged even more artists to move to Taos, which, in turn, increased the number of visitors who came to town to buy art or simply to look at it—while spending money at the restaurants, hotels, bars and gift shops. This trend has continued—Taos today is a major art center in the U.S. with dozens of art galleries and tourist-related shops.

The historic, as well as artistic, aspects of Taos were promoted by Mabel. Her artist friends painted people, places and events connected to the local Spanish and Native American cultures. These paintings, and the media attention given to the historic aspects of the town, helped spread the fame of Taos.

Today, Mabel's house and her grave, in the historic Kit Carson Cemetery, are two of many attractions that tourists visit when they come to town.

It is difficult to imagine what Taos would be like today had Mabel Dodge Luhan not taken up residence there in 1917. For 45 years, her promotion of the little town gave it worldwide fame. Artists, historians, writers and tourists began to visit Taos. Each year, the number of visitors—and social and cultural events, art galleries and historic tours—increases, thanks to the influence of Mabel Dodge Luhan.

As you read any article, you'll notice, of course, that certain words appear repeatedly. Rather than write them down again and again during your note taking, develop an easy-to-use shorthand for the article and write a key to it across the top of the page.

For instance, in this article, the author uses several terms that can be easily abbreviated: M (for Mabel Dodge Luhan—you didn't write MDL, did you?); T (Taos); a&w (artists and writers); a (art); NA (Native American).

Here's what my notes might look like:

1. intro —ovrvw M on T
   —brt a&w, stayd

2. social —top dog
   —salon
   —a&w brt a&w
   —a scene

3. cult. —hist. Sp/NA
   —hse/gr

4. conc. —wht lke w/o M?
   —M's effect
   —yrly vsts incr./M

Which, if you can't understand it, translates as:

1. Introduction
   A. Overview of Mabel Dodge Luhan's influence on Taos.
   B. She brought artists and writers to visit, some of whom then moved there.

2. Social effects
   A. Mabel was the head of "society" in Taos.
   B. She created a "salon" atmosphere in her home.
   C. Her friends, the famous artists and writers, brought other artists and writers to Taos—and to Mabel.

3. Cultural effects
   A. Historic aspects, especially the promotion of the Native American and Spanish cultures.

B. Her own house and grave today are part of the historic/cultural scene.

4. Conclusion
   A. Taos wouldn't be the same without her.
   B. Thanks to her, it's a bustling town today filled with artistic residents and visitors.
   C. The cultural and social scene—which she developed—continues to increase in numbers and importance.

Getting it all down

Now, read the next article and take notes on it using the method outlined above. Then, compare what you've written with the sample notes I've included following it.

Whither South Africa?

The bickering that has gone on among both white and black South African dissidents, primarily over whether to boycott that country's first free elections, is reminiscent of the playground squabbles we went through as children. Bosom buddies one moment, down-in-the-dirt antagonists the next, back in class again minutes later.

Is such bickering merely a method of negotiation, a way for each of the sides, but primarily the African National Congress and the Zulu nationalists, to convince the other that unless their demands are met, they may well scuttle the entire process? Again, is it not like the child who, denied the field at first base, takes his ball and goes home, allowing pride to overcome his desire to play ball, no matter what position he is given?

Perhaps, but the real passions that lie behind such brinkmanship cannot be denied. And neither can the very real sense that for many of the "players," there is far more emotion at work than political maneuvering or logic.

Most of the citizenry is tired of the daily deadlines, the factionalism, the ever-changing alliances, enemies turning into friends overnight, friends waking up enemies. Breakthroughs are announced in newspapers' morning editions only to be proved false by the evening.

This disarray has in many cases overshadowed the active campaigning by Nelson Mandela's African National Congress and President F. W. de Klerk's National Party, the two major factions in the election. Their campaign has been further eroded by the party that has, so far at least, opted out of the elections altogether—the Zulu nationalists' Inkatha Freedom Party. It is unthinkable that they and their mercurial leader, Mangosuthu G. Buthelezi, will hold themselves out of the election process entirely. They simply have too much to lose—patronage, credibility and the ability to incorporate their own platform in the newly formed government—to boycott the elections entirely.

But Buthelezi and his party have defied logic and done the unthinkable before. While many observers believe his holdout to be a shrewd strategic move, one that will enable him to extract every possible conces-sion before he enters the electoral fray, others remember his withdrawal from negotiations last year that many feel would have enabled him to displace de

Klerk as the titular opposition leader and expand his influence beyond the predominantly Zulu province of Natal. Instead, he became even more insular and isolated, scared off many former supporters and lost the votes of many who were ready to make him the alternative to Mandela and the ANC.

Applying the system

How closely do your notes resemble something like this?

Bick in SA

I.   Boyct? Neg ploy by ANC/Z?
II. Real pass—> emtn/pol mnvring
III. Cits no lke chngs, factionsm, dly deads
IV. Bick ovrshdws cam.—2 maj facts (ANC/NM, Natl P/DK).
V.   Z-I-MB-OUT? 2 mch lse?
VI. MB strat? CF prev withd neg. Cd hv displcd DK. But isol, scrd sups, lst vts ANC.

Another exercise: What's the question?

Of course, reading in this way will make your notes that much more succinct and valuable, as will another device for making yourself a more active reader: asking yourself questions about the material. For example:

- What are the most important points in the section I've just read?
- What information from this section is my instructor likely to ask about in the next exam?

- What important theories/ideas from my other reading
  are covered, explained or expanded here?

As you read the text, try thinking of note-taking as just
writing down the answers to questions about the material.

For instance, let's take a look at this brief passage, adapted
from the article, "Days of Trauma and Fear," which appeared in
the April 4, 1994 edition of *Time*:

> Mexico is not a seamless unity but a mosaic of
> dissimilar people afforded unequal progress. Only
> the top half has joined the 20th century; the rest is
> mired in unyielding poverty. Until recently, infla-
> tion was at 50% and, despite a number of federal
> initiatives, the gap between rich and poor continues
> to widen: The poorest Mexicans' share of the
> national income de-clined from 5% eight years ago
> to 4.3% today.
>
> Others are taking advantage of Mexico's grow-
> ing clout in global markets and getting rich in the
> bargain. Mexico's gross domestic product has
> grown from $2,525 per capita just four years ago to
> $4,324 last year. But, as we've already seen, these
> encouraging statistics mask a situation that makes
> Mexico one of the most unequal countries in the
> world.
>
> The recent assassination of leading presidential
> candidate Luis Donaldo Colosio, the ruling party's
> handpicked successor to President Carlos Salinas
> de Gortari, crippled the confidence of the country
> striving to climb the slippery ladder to "First
> World" nation status. The murder was only the
> latest blow in a year that has featured violent

rebellion in the southern state of Chiapas led by the Zapatista National Liberation Army, economic uncertainty and political disruption at a time when many citizens thought they had finally achieved a semblance of stability, peace and prosperity.

The Mexican stock market reacted violently, even for a market for which the word volatile would normally be an understatement—plunging 100 points soon after opening, though it closed the day down less than one-percent.

The author is throwing around a handful of statistics and a few mouthfuls of Hispanic names in describing the current state of the economy in Mexico.

Should we remember the statistics about per capita income, poor Mexicans' share of income, the stock market loss? Should these statistics appear in our notes?

If we read linearly, starting at the beginning and plodding along to the last word, we probably would be tempted to write down these numbers and what they mean in our notes. But taking the article as a whole, it can readily be summarized without really worrying about the numbers: "Mexico's been having problems, is a very unequal society, the assassination has probably made it all worse."

Therefore, the statistics are not especially important, but the enormity of the problem to which they give credence *is*. The names bring up the same problem (and solution) dealt with in the South African article: Whenever possible, simplify and just note, somewhere, your abbreviations. Just as I substituted ANC for African National Congress, NM for Nelson Mandela, DK for de Klerk, and so on, so you should abbreviate Luis Donaldo Colosio, Carlos Salinas de Gortari, Chiapas and the Zapatista National Liberation Army. These are the terms most likely to be repeated again and again in any article on the current political or economic situation in Mexico.

A note on primary sources

Primary sources (what *Freud* said, rather than what some textbook author *says* he said) present some unique note-taking challenges.

While textbooks give you digested information, primary sources require you to do more work to get to the heart of the matter. In the sciences (social and physical), literary criticism, history and philosophy, original thinkers will present assertions and findings. They might suggest new theories or other explanations of events or phenomena. And, in doing any of the above, they will very likely support or seek to disprove established beliefs and theories.

Your notes on primary source documents should summarize the author's assertions. Under each of these summaries, you should make notes on the arguments and evidence the author presents in support of these conclusions.

The process here can be similar to that outlined previously. You can first skim the document to see what the author is presenting that's truly *new* (or, at least, was new when he wrote it), and then go back to see how he proves these claims.

For instance, if you are assigned *Thus Spake Zarathustra* by Nietzsche in your Philosophy 101 course, the headings in your notes might be:

1. The dominant force in history is the "will to power."

2. A "transvaluation of values" is necessary to produce a system of morality that produces greatness rather than goodness.

Take Notes

3. Blending Dionysian instinct with Apollonian reason and ethics will result in the "Ubermensch" (Superman).
4. Democracy promotes conformity and suppresses excellence.
5. God is dead.

You could easily gather these by skimming the text—because of Nietzsche's tendency to use aphorisms—or by reading a good introduction to it. Then, as you read the text more thoroughly, you'd want to note how the philosopher supports these assertions.

In this chapter, I pointed out some of the components to look for when taking notes from reading assignments, and touched on one of the most important tools to help you get down the material in an organized manner. In the next, I'll give your an even more powerful tool—outlining.

Chapter Seven

OUTLINES AND OTHER TOOLS

I have a confession to make: To this very day, I resent having to write an outline for a book, article or research project. I'd much rather (and do) just sit down and start writing.

Even though I know that doing an outline is a great way to organize my thoughts so that I can write more quickly, it just seems to take more time that I could spend actually *writing*.

Well, I would have hated myself in school if I knew then what I know now: You should do outlines while you are *reading,* as well.

Outlines will help you review a text more quickly and remember it more clearly.

And outlining texts will make you a *better* writer.

Many students underline in their textbooks or use magic markers to "highlight" them. This is a sure sign of masochism, as it guarantees only one thing: They will have to read a great deal of the deadly book again when they review for their exams.

Others write notes in the margin. This is a little bit better as a strategy for getting better grades, but marginalia usually make the most sense only in context, so this messy method also forces the student to reread a great deal of text.

What's *the* most effective way to read and remember your textbooks? *(Sigh.)* Yes, the outline.

Reverse engineering

Outlining a textbook, article or other secondary source is a little bit like what the Japanese call "reverse engineering"—a way of developing a schematic for something so that you can see exactly how it's been put together. Seeing how published authors build their arguments and marshal their research will help you when it comes time to write your own papers.

Seeing that logic of construction will also help you a great deal in remembering the book—by putting the author's points down in *your* words, you will be building a way to retrieve the key points of the book more easily from your memory.

What's more, outlining will force you to distinguish the most important points from those of secondary importance, helping you build a true understanding of the topic.

The bare bones of outlining

Standard outlines use Roman numerals (I, II, III, etc.), capital letters, Arabic numerals (1, 2, 3, 4...), and lower-case letters and indentations to show relationship and importance of topics in the text. While you certainly don't have to use the Roman-numeral system, your outline should be organized in the following manner:

Title
Author

I. First important topic in the text
  A. First subtopic
    1. First subtopic of A
      a. First subtopic of 1
      b. Second subtopic of 1
    2. Second subtopic of A
II. The second important topic in the text

Get the idea? In a book, the Roman numerals usually would refer to chapters; the capital letters to subheadings; and the Arabic numbers and lower-case letters to blocks of paragraphs. In an article or single chapter, the Roman numbers would correspond to subheadings, capital letters to blocks of paragraphs, Arabic numerals to paragraphs, small letters to key sentences.

What's he getting at?

We understand things in outline form. Ask an intelligent person to recount something and he'll state the main points and only enough details to make his words interesting and understandable.

The discipline of creating outlines will help you zero in on the most important points an author is making and capture them, process them, and, thereby, retain them.

Sometimes an author will have the major point of a paragraph in the first sentence. But just as often the main idea of a paragraph or section will follow some of these telltale words: therefore, because, thus, since, as a result.

When we see these words we should identify the material they introduce as the major points in our outline. The material immediately preceding and following almost always will be in support of these major points. The outline is an extraordinary tool for organizing your thoughts and your time.

Let's practice what we're preaching

Turn to chapter 10, which is an excerpt from the new second edition of my own *101 Great Answers to the Toughest Interview Questions* (Career Press, 1994) and then outline it. Let's see how well you've been paying attention!

Create a time line

I always found it frustrating to read textbooks in social studies. I'd go through chapters on France, England, the Far East, and have a fairly good understanding of those areas, but have no idea where certain events stood in a global context.

To help overcome that difficulty, consider drawing a time line that you can update periodically. The time line will help you visualize the chronology and remember the relationship of key world events.

For instance, a time line for the earliest years in the history of the United States might look like this (I would suggest a horizontal time line, but the layout of this book makes reproducing it that way difficult. So here's a vertical version):

1776————	The American Revolution
1783————	The Articles of Confederation
1786————	Shay's Rebellion
1789————	Ratification of the Constitution
1791————	The Federal Reserve Bank
1795————	The XYZ Affair
1798————	The Alien and Sedition Laws

Comparing this to other timelines in your notebook would put these events in the context of the end of the Napoleonic Era and the French Revolution.

Draw a concept tree

Another terrific device for limiting the amount of verbiage in your notes and making them more memorable is the concept tree. Like a time line, the concept tree is a visual representation of the relationship among several key facts. For instance, one might depict the system of government in the United States this way:

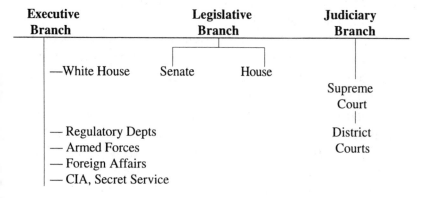

Now we can give credence to the old saying, "A picture is worth a thousand words," since time lines and concept trees will be much more helpful than mere words in remembering material, particularly conceptual material. And developing them will ensure that your interest in the text will not flag too much.

Add a vocabulary list

Many questions on exams require students to define the terminology in a discipline. Your physics professor will want to

Take Notes

know what "vectors" are, your calculus teacher will want to know about "differential equations," your history professor will want you to be well versed on "The Cold War," and your English Lit professor will require you to know about the "Romantic Poets."

As you read your textbook, be sure to write down all new terms that seem important and their definitions. I used to draw a box around terms and definitions in my notes, because I knew these were among the most likely items to be asked about and the box would draw my attention to them when I was reviewing.

Most textbooks will provide definitions of key terms. However, if you look back to the article on economics we studied in Chapter 6, you'll see that the author did *not* explicitly state a definition of the "trickle-down" theory, for example, but that it *could* be inferred from the text.

This is an important point: Even if your textbook does not define a key term, make sure you write the term down in your notes *with* a definition. It will be much harder months later to remember what the term means.

In addition, even if the author does provide a definition, your notes should reflect *your* understanding of the term. Take the time to rephrase and write it in your own words. This will help you remember it.

I would also recommend writing down examples for terms that you might have trouble remembering. If you're reading an English textbook and you come across the term "oxymoron," which is defined by the author as "a figure of speech combining seemingly contradictory expressions," wouldn't it be better if your notes on figures of speech read something like this?

oxymoron:	jumbo shrimp, cruel kindness
onomatopoeia:	PLOP, PLOP, FIZZ, FIZZ
metaphor:	food for thought
simile:	this is *like* that

Wait, you're not done yet

After you've finished making notes on a chapter, go through them and identify the most important points, which are the ones that might turn up on tests, either with an asterisk or by highlighting them. You'll probably end up marking about 40 to 50 percent of your entries. When you're reviewing for a test, you should *read* all of the notes, but your asterisks will indicate which points you considered the most important while the chapter was very fresh in your mind.

To summarize, when it comes to taking notes from your texts or other reading material, you should:

- Take a cursory look through the chapter before you begin reading. Look for subheads, highlighted terms and summaries to give you a sense of the content.
- Read each section thoroughly. While your review of the chapter "clues" will help your understanding of the material, you should read for comprehension rather than speed.
- Make notes immediately after you've finished reading, using mapping, the outline, time line, concept tree and vocabulary list methods of organization as necessary.
- Mark with an asterisk or highlight the key points as you review your notes.

The advice in this chapter will help you remember the books that you have to carry back and forth to school all too often. Believe it or not, that's a luxury. When you have term papers to do, you'll be forced to use books that you cannot remove from the library. The next chapter will tell you how to make sure you get all of the necessary information from them with the fewest trips to the stacks.

Chapter Eight

NOTES ON LIBRARY MATERIALS

Sometime during your high school or college years, you will undoubtedly be called upon to do some extensive research, either for a term paper or some other major project. Such a task will indeed be a major undertaking. And note-taking will be only one aspect of the process, albeit an important one.

(While I will give you a terrific system for taking notes for a term paper or report in this chapter, I urge you to also read *Write Papers,* another helpful book in my **HOW TO STUDY Program,** which thoroughly covers *all* the important steps, from selecting a topic and developing an outline to researching and taking notes to writing, rewriting and proofreading your final paper.)

As you will discover, writing a term paper will require you to take notes from a number of sources, most of them available at the library. But the more periodicals, reference books and even microfiche you uncover as terrific sources of information for your project, the more likely you'll be told you won't be able to take much of this material out of the library. You'll have to take your notes *at the library,* not at your leisure in the comfort of your room.

So you'll definitely want a note-taking system that is quick, thorough, efficient and precludes the necessity of having to return to the source *again.* What's the answer?

No, it's not photocopying.

While technology should provide convenience, it should never become a substitute for skill. Calculators should make it easier to add and divide and multiply, but we should never forget how to perform these functions without them.

Likewise, photocopying machines should make it easy for us to reproduce extensive passages from books and journals, but they should never be thought of as a substitute for taking good notes.

The reasons are similar to the arguments against tape-recording lectures that we made earlier. Photocopying does not save time—it only ensures that you will have to read materials again to unearth the most important facts from them.

Why photocopying is redundant

You've found a resource that's perfect for your term paper. Your first impulse might be to find the library photocopying machine and pump some quarters into it.

Is photocopying a help or a hindrance?

I used to employ a "system" of photocopying when preparing for my term papers. I would go to the library with nothing except a roll of dimes (photocopying was a lot cheaper in those days), and comb the card catalog, the stacks and the periodicals index for possible sources, using the library-supplied pencils to write the information down on call slips. I'd stack the volumes and periodicals around me at one of the tables and comb through them for hours, looking for juicy quotes and fun factoids.

I'd mark the books with those handy call slips. Then, I'd haul all of the useful sources over to the photocopier and begin xeroxing away my hard-earned money.

I'd wind up going home with a pile of photostats that I had to read (and, as for the material, *reread*), which I'd do armed with pens of as many different colors as I could find. I'd underline all of the related passages with the same color, pick up another pen and go sifting through the photocopies again. This method certainly helped me produce some darned good papers, but it also ensured that I spent too much time rereading information, organizing and reorganizing the research before I ever began actually writing.

I'm about to save you a lot of grief by letting you in on one of the greatest card tricks you've ever seen. And, by the way, you won't ever have to wait in line for the photocopying machine at the library again.

Become a "poINDEXter"

When I was in school, we called the smart kids "Poindexters" (probably one of the nicest things we called them). Well, the root of Poindexter is *index*, and the smart kids' secret to writing effective term papers with the least effort, it just so happens, was index cards.

While that metaphor was a bit of a stretch, it's not an exaggeration to say that index cards will cut the time it takes to research and organize a term paper in half.

Here's how they work:

As you'll learn when you read **Write Papers,** developing a preliminary outline is an important early step in the paper-writing process. Assuming you have completed this step, you would then be prepared to gather information for your term paper or research project. Proceed to your local stationery store and buy a supply of 3 x 5 note cards.

As you review each source, you'll discover some are packed with helpful information, while others may have no useful material at all. Once you determine that you will use a source, make a working bibliography card:

- ***In the upper right-hand corner of the card***: Write the library call number (Dewey decimal or Library of Congress number), or any other detail that will help you locate the material (e.g., "Science Reading Room," "Main Stacks, 3rd Floor," etc.).

- ***On the main part of the card:*** Write the author's name, if one is given, last name first. Include the title of the article, if applicable, and write and underline the name of the book, magazine or other publication. In addition, include any other details, such as date of publication, edition, volume number or page numbers where the article or information was found.

- ***In the upper left-hand corner:*** Number the card—the card for the first source you plan to use, for example, is #1, the second, #2, and so on. If you accidently skip a number or end up not using a source for which you've filled out a card, don't worry. It's only important that you assign a different number to each card.

- ***At the bottom of the card:*** Write the name of the library (if you're working at more than one) at which you found the source.

By filling out a card for each source, you have just created your ***working bibliography***—a listing of all your sources that

Take Notes

will be an invaluable tool when you have to prepare the final bibliography for your term paper.

Sample Bibliography Card For A Book

```
(1)                                        315.6
                        Main Reading Room

             Jones, Karen A.

     The Life and Times of Bob Smith.
            (see esp. pp. 43-48)

               Card Catalog
            Main Street Library
```

Sample Bibliography Card For A Magazine Article

```
(2)                        Periodical Room

                 Perkins, Stan
      "The Life and Times of Bob Smith"
                Smith Magazine
         (April 24, 1989; pp. 22-26)

               Readers' Guide
              University Library
```

Sample Bibliography Card For A Newspaper Article

---

(3)   Microfiche Room

Black, Bill
"Bob Smith: The New Widget Spinner"
<u>New York Times</u>
(June 16, 1976, late edition, p. A12)

New York Times Index
Main Street Library

Shuffling cards is a good deal

With index cards, you can organize your list of resources in different ways, just by shuffling the deck.

For example, you might want to start by organizing your cards by resource: magazine articles, encyclopedias, books, newspapers, etc. Then, when you're in the magazine room of the library, you will have a quick and easy way to make sure you read all your magazine articles at the same time. Ditto for your trip to the newspaper reading room, the reference shelf and so on.

But at some point, you might want to have your list of resources organized in alphabetical order. Or separated into piles of resources you've checked and those you haven't. No problem: Just shuffle your cards again.

Even with the help of a computer, it would be time-consuming to do all of this on paper. The notecard system is neater and more efficient. And that's the key to getting your work done as quickly and painlessly as possible!

I guarantee you'll win *this* card game

You're sitting in the library, now, surrounded by a veritable bonanza of source materials for your paper. You've completed your bibliography cards. It's time to take notes. Here's how:

Write one thought, idea, quote or fact—and **only** *one—on each card.* No exceptions. If you encounter a very long quote or string of data, you can write on both the front and back of the card, if necessary. But *never* carry over a note to a second card. If you have an uncontrollable urge to do that, the quote is too long. If you feel that the author is making an incredibly good point, paraphrase it.

Write in your own words. Don't copy material word for word—you may inadvertently wind up plagiarizing when you write. Summarize key points or restate the material in your own words.

Put quotation marks around any material copied verbatim. Sometimes an author makes a point so perfectly, so poetically, you *do* want to capture it exactly as is. It's fine to do this on a limited basis. But when you do so, you must copy such statements *exactly*—every sentence, every word, every comma should be precisely as written in the original. And make sure you put quotation marks around this material. Don't rely on your memory to recall, later, which copy was paraphrased and which you copied verbatim.

Put the number of the corresponding bibliography card in the upper-left corner. This is the number you put in the upper-left-hand corner of the bibliography card.

Include the page numbers (where you found the information) on the card. You can add this information under the resource number.

Write down the topic letter that corresponds to your preliminary outline. For example, the second section, "B," of your preliminary outline is about the French withdrawal from Vietnam. You find an interesting quote from a United States official that refers to this withdrawal. Write down the topic letter "B" in the upper right-hand corner of your note card. (If you're not sure, mark the card with an asterisk [*] or other symbol instead. Later, when you have a more detailed outline, you may discover where it fits.)

Give it a headline. Next to the topic letter, add a brief description of the information on the card. For example, your note card with the quote about the French withdrawal may read, "French Withdrawal: U.S. Comments."

As you fill out your note cards, be sure to transfer information accurately. Double-check names, dates and other statistics. The beauty of using the note-card system is that, once you've captured the information you need, you should never have to return to any of the sources a second time.

A note of caution here: While this system is terrific for helping you organize your time and material, don't allow it to hamstring you if you find other interesting material.

For instance, you might come across interesting quotes or statistics that could add flavor and authority to your term paper, but you're not quite sure where they will fit in. Put an asterisk on the card; return to it later.

Take Notes

As with the other exercises in note-taking, the index card system requires you not to be a *copyist*—you could have used the photostat machine for that—but a *processor of information.*

Constantly ask yourself questions while looking at the source material:

Is the author saying this in such a way that I want to quote her directly, or should I just paraphrase the material?

If you decide to paraphrase, you obviously don't have to write down the author's exact verbiage, and, therefore, can re-sort to some of the note-taking tips discussed in other chapters. The answer to this question, in other words, will have a big impact on how much time it takes to fill in each index card.

Does this material support or contradict the arguments or facts of another author?

Which one of them do I believe? If there *is* contradictory evidence, should I note it? Can I refute it? If it supports the material I already have, is it interesting or redundant?

Where does this material fit into my outline?

Often, source material won't be as sharply delineated as your plan for the term paper, which is why it is important to place *one and only one* thought on each card. Even though an author might place more than one thought into a paragraph, or even a sentence, you will be able to stick to your organizational guns if you keep your cards close to the outline vest.

You'll be superorganized

Before I came up with any term-paper research system in high school, my student life was, quite literally, a mess. I had pages and pages of notes for term papers, but sometimes I was unsure where quotes came from and whether or not they were direct quotes or paraphrases.

My photocopy "system" wasn't much of an improvement. Often, I would forget one piece of the bibliographic information I needed, necessitating yet another last-minute trip to the library. And organizing the voluminous notes when it came time to put my thoughts in order was worse than the researching and writing itself.

The card system will save you all of that grief. Writing one thought, idea, quote, etc. per card will eliminate the problems caused when disparate pieces of information appear on the same piece of paper. And writing the number of the source down before doing anything else will help you avoid any problems relating to proper attribution.

When you're ready to do your final outline, all you'll need to do is organize and reorder your cards until you have the most effective flow.

This simple note-card system is, in fact, one that many professional writers—including this one—swear by long after they leave the world of term papers and class reports behind.

Chapter Nine

TAKING GREAT NOTES FOR ORAL REPORTS

The English poet John Donne wrote, "Death be not proud," and no wonder: In many public opinion polls in which respondents were asked to rate their biggest fears, public speaking—and *not* the good old grim reaper—won...hands down.

This leads one to wonder why there haven't been more horror films made about standing up in front of an audience than about ax murderers. And makes anyone who has done a considerable amount of public speaking wonder why more people simply don't do the sensible thing to overcome their fear of "lecternship"—prepare and practice.

Researching, taking and properly using notes, and re-hearsing, should ensure that you will have nothing but a mild case of the butterflies before you have to get up in front of your classmates, professors or any other audience, friendly or otherwise.

Good notes are your lifeline when you stand up to say what's on your mind. They should act as cues to remind you where your talk should go next, and they should make you feel secure that you can get through the ordeal.

However, the *wrong* kind of notes can be a crutch that guarantees not success, but audience boredom. You've probably seen any number of people get up in front of an audience and just read some papers they have in front of them.

Is there any *better* cure for insomnia?

Let me say a few—very few—words

Exactly what sort of talk is this going to be? Odds are, if you've been assigned to give a talk for a class, it will fall into one of the following categories:

- *Exposition*—a rather straightforward statement of facts.
- An *argument,* with which you are trying to change the opinions of at least a portion of the audience.
- A *description* that will provide a visual picture to your listeners.
- *Narration*—or storytelling.

The most common forms of oral reports assigned in school will be the exposition and argument. You'll find that you will research and organize your information for these types of speeches pretty much the way you would a term paper. So, review Chapter 8 (and, again, read **Write Papers**).

A note of caution: If you're preparing an *argument*, don't convince yourself you don't have to research *both* sides of the topic just because you're only presenting *one* of them. You should be doubly prepared with all the facts, as you might be challenged with questions or the arguments of other speakers.

Take Notes

As you gather information for your report, making notes on index cards as you did for your term paper, keep this in mind: In order for you to be effective, you must use some different techniques when you *tell* your story rather than *write* it. Here are a few:

- *Don't make your topic too broad.* This advice, offered for preparing written reports as well, is even more important when preparing a talk. Try giving an effective speech on "Bill Clinton," "South Africa" or "Shakespeare"...in 15 minutes, frequently the amount of time assigned for oral reports. These topics are more suited to a series of books!

  "How Shakespeare portrays Hamlet As The Mad Prince" or "How Clinton Weathered New Hampshire" or "The Role of the Inkatha Freedom Party in South Africa's Elections" are more manageable. Narrowing the scope of your talk will help you research and organize it more effectively.

- *Don't overuse statistics.* While they're very important for lending credibility to your position, too many will only weigh down your speech and bore your audience—as presidential debates can usually be counted on to do.

- *Anecdotes add color and life to your talk.* But use them sparingly, because they can slow down your speech. Get to the punchline before the yawns start.

- *Be careful with quotes.* Unlike a term paper, a speech allows you to establish yourself as an authority with less fear of being accused of plagiarism. So you can present a lot more facts without attribution. (But you'd better have the sources in case you're asked about your facts.) You can use quotes, though, when they contain distinctive language or elicit an emotion. Be sure to attribute the source.

How to organize your talk for maximum effect

I've done so much public speaking throughout my career that I've actually grown to enjoy it—in fact, I look forward to talking to a room full of strangers. I don't think that would be the case at all were it not for a piece of valuable advice I acquired quite a few years ago:

> There is only one best way to organize a speech:
> Tell them what you are going to say; say it; then,
> tell them what you said.

An outline for a speech is going to be different than one for a term paper, because of the way effective presentations must be organized. Unlike readers, your listeners will not have a piece of paper in front of them to ponder and review. Your classmates and teacher will be relying on ear and memory to make sense of your talk, so you will have to be somewhat repetitious, though, hopefully, in a barely noticeable way.

When organizing your facts for your talk, you can use the same method—the index cards—as you used in preparing your term paper. But as you put together your outline, follow my advice: Tell them what you're going to say, say it, then tell them what you said. It's that simple.

Create your outline

Now that you have the information and colorful quotes you need to make a convincing speech, start organizing it. Go

Take Notes

through your cards and decide the best way to arrange them so that they build toward a convincing argument. Then, using the order you've established, go through the cards and develop an outline.

Let's say you were assigned to take one side of the argument, "Should drugs be legalized?" Your outline might look like this:

The Opening

I. Drugs should be legalized
II. This will help solve, not deepen, the drug crisis in this country
III. Keeping drugs illegal assures that criminals get rich and government funds get wasted

The Middle

I. The reasons to legalize drugs
   A. Artificially inflated prices
      1. Costs are inflated 2,500 percent
   B. Public funds are being wasted
      1. Law enforcement is not working
      2. Funds for rehabilitation are paltry
      3. Education funds are inadequate
II. Control would be easier
   A. It has worked in other countries
   B. Licensing would increase revenues
   C. Harsh penalties would curb sales to minors
   D. Drug addicts would be known and available for counseling
III. Prohibition doesn't work
   A. Statistics to support statement
   B. Parallels with Roaring Twenties

The Closing

I.   The costly, ineffective War on Drugs
II. Legalization sounds radical, but it would work
III. The alternative is far more dangerous

As you can see, the speech will restate the same points three times as a way of emphasizing them and assuring that they will be remembered.

Learning to fly without a net

Now read through it several times. Read it to yourself to make sure you haven't left out any important facts or arguments. Then read it aloud to see how it flows, fixing as necessary.

Now, it's time to go without a net. Stand in front of the mirror and try giving the speech, start to finish, looking at nothing but your own beautiful face. But have your notes close by.

How did you do? What parts of the speech did you remember with no trouble? Where did you stumble? If you're like 99 percent of the human race, you probably had to wrench your eyes from the mirror now and then to look at your notes.

Of course, you're not ready for an audience yet. Nor should you expect to be at this point. You'll want to practice many more times before you face your listeners. The purpose of this exercise is to help you identify what areas you really know— and which are going to require a little prompting.

Your next step is to distill your talk even further on additional note cards. For those areas with which you're most familiar, the ones you remember without looking at your notes, jot down a simple phrase, even a symbol, that prompts you to continue with your talk. For those details you're a little unsure of, write as much detail as you need. As you continue to practice speaking, you should further distill the information on your note cards, until what you have is the barest framework possible.

My advice for preparing your final note cards is much like the advice that veteran travelers offer on packing for a long trip: Put only the bare necessities in your suitcase. Then, take half of them out.

The mistakes novices make...and you shouldn't

This all makes giving an oral report sound scary, doesn't it. It certainly did to me at one time. I took a course on public speaking at the American Management Association, one of the leading providers of continuing adult education. Since I made my living with printed words, I wanted to have lots of them in front of me so I wouldn't feel naked. I'd hide behind my legal pad!

But the instructor, to whom I've been grateful countless times since, would allow us to bring only three index cards for a three-minute talk. And each card could have no more than 10 words written on it.

Certainly many students in the class stumbled, but they probably hadn't rehearsed. On the other hand, I guarantee you that, as a relative novice at public speaking, you will make one (and maybe all) of these "Big Three" mistakes if you bring your entire text with you:

- You will read from it, failing to make eye contact with your audience. This will help to ensure that you lose their interest and your credibility. How familiar can you be with a subject if you have to read your entire speech?
- If you stop reading for a second to ad lib or look at your listeners, you will lose your place. It's much harder to find that key word that will jog your memory on a full page of text than on an index card.

- You won't be familiar enough with your speech, because, after all, you'll have it there with you, so why bother rehearsing or memorizing anything?

As I've become more polished as a public speaker, I've noticed that having only the cards has encouraged me to ad lib more. And, by and large, these are the most well received parts of the speech. Talking relatively freely, with the help of only the sparest notes, is one way to make sure the "real you" comes through.

And that's who the audience is there to hear, right?

Please take note

I've begun to think of my notes for speeches as the purest form of the craft we've described in this book. You are distilling ideas down to a phrase, a word, a number, perhaps just a symbol that will help you remember under pressure.

Often, the very *process* of taking notes is enough, in itself, to ensure that a fact, an impression or a formula, will last in your memory for a long time. Note-taking is stripping data down to its essence.

Although I've made many suggestions about the best way to take notes, remember that it is a very individualistic and pragmatic art. Each of you should figure out what works best for you, then refine your technique using the suggestions made in these chapters. It will be worth the effort.

In the next chapter, I've reproduced an excerpt from one of my other books—***101 Great Answers to the Toughest Interview Questions, 2nd Edition***—on which to practice your newly mastered note-taking and outlining skills. And I've shown my own outline of the chapter, too. Just don't peek at my notes before you take your own!

Chapter Ten

LET'S PRACTICE WHAT WE'VE PREACHED

Starting on the next page, I've reprinted an excerpt (most of chapter 2) from the second edition of my book, *101 Great Anwers to the Toughest Interview Questions.*

Practice outlining it (see chapter 7) and taking notes on it. You'll soon see how well you learned the lessons of this book—or what chapters you need to go back and reread!

On pages 115 and 116, I've given you two blank pages to fill in your outline. On pages 117 and 118, I've reproduced my own. Don't peek until you finish yours! See how close you get to this "model" (though it's certainly not the only "solution"). And note that I've written out much more of it than I normally would (as opposed to applying my own shorthand), purely for the sake of readability.

If you find you have a lot of trouble with this exercise, forget what I said about linear reading—go back and read *Take Notes* again, from start to finish!

What You're Up Against

The days of filling out the standard application and chat-ting your way through one or two interviews are gone. These days, interviewers and hiring managers are reluctant to leave anything to chance. Many have begun to experiment with the latest techniques for data-gathering and analysis. For employers, interviewing has gone from an art to a full-fledged science.

Does this make you feel like a specimen under a microscope? Get used to it. Times are tougher for companies, so it's natural to assume that interviews will be tougher for their prospective employees.

In the many years I've subscribed to human resources journals, I've noticed an increasing number of new interviewing methods developed to help interviewers measure, as accurately as possible, how well prospective candidates would perform on the job. The "database interview," the "situational interview," and the "stress (confrontational) interview" are only a few of the special treatments you might en-counter on your way to landing the ideal job.

The good news is that companies hoping to survive in our new service economy will depend on the human element—you—as their most valuable business asset. But because there are more "humans" competing for fewer jobs, employers will be focused on hiring only the very best applicants.

Interviewing has always been a challenge. But these days it is serious business. Consider:

The incredible shrinking company. Rampant downsizing has left fewer jobs. At the same time, the "cost of hire"—the amount of money it takes to land a suitable candidate for a job—has escalated dramatically in recent years.

From business suit to lawsuit. Lawsuits against employers for wrongful discharge and other employment-related causes have also increased exponentially over the past decade. Hiring mistakes can be costly, making it more important than ever for companies to be sure the people they do hire will be right for the job.

The great cattle call. Although the labor force is indeed shrinking as a result of the much ballyhooed "baby bust," you're liable to face a new kind of competition as a job applicant. These days, you can expect to bump into fellow candidates at every level of experience on the way to or from your first interview—or your fourth.

Where Does That Leave You?

More employers seem to be looking for a special kind of employee—someone with experience, confidence and the initiative to learn what he or she needs to know. Someone who requires very little supervision. Someone with a hands-on attitude—from beginning to end.

Since it's difficult to tell all that from an application and handshake, here's what's happening:

Passing the test(s). You'll probably have to go through more interviews than your predecessors for the same job—no matter what your level of expertise. Knowledge and experience still give you an inside edge. But these days, you'll need stamina, too. Your honesty, your intelligence, your mental health—even the toxicity of your blood—may be measured before you can be considered fully assessed.

Braving more interviews. You may also have to tiptoe through a mine field of different types of interview situations—and keep your head—to survive as a new hire.

Don't go out and subscribe to a human resources journal. Just do all you can to remain confident and flexible—and ready with your answers. No matter what kind of interview you find yourself in, this approach should carry you through with flying colors.

Let's take a brief no-consequences tour of the interview circuit.

Level One: The Screening Interview

If you're pursuing a job at a mid-size or large company (any organization of more than 250 employees), your first interview is likely to begin in the human resources department.

What can you expect? Let's say you're applying for your dream job as a middle manager at ABC Widget Co. Arriving on time for your first interview, you're greeted by Heather.

Heather is a lower-level person in the human resources department. She's been given a bare-bones introduction to the duties and responsibilities you must have to operate successfully in the position you're after. If she's not completely up to speed, it's probably not her fault. The person who will manage this new position (the hiring manager) may not have had time to fill out a detailed position description, or to tell Heather exactly what he or she is looking for.

Regardless of how much she's got to go on, Heather's job is pretty simple: weed out the number of candidates whose resumes jibe with the short version of the job description, so that the hiring manager will have fewer candidates to interview.

After you've gotten through the preliminaries, Heather is likely to follow a script. She will ask questions to see if you have the qualifications for the position: the appropriate degree, the right amount of experience, a willingness to relocate, and so on.

Heather will be trying to determine whether you've been completely truthful on your resume. Did you work where and when you claim? Have the titles and responsibilities you're bragging about? Make the salaries you've stated?

Take Notes

The screening interview may also drift into a few qualitative areas. Does she think you're sufficiently enthusiastic? Do you sound intelligent? Exhibit any obvious emotional disturbances? Are you articulate? Energetic? Are you the type of person who would fit well within the department, and the company?

Getting Past the Gate

If you pass the screening hurdle, Heather may resort to an arsenal of professional interviewing techniques. Remember, Heather is trained and practiced in the science of interviewing.

While it's still up to the hiring manager to decide whether you'll still be checking the classified ads next week, Heather has the power, at this point, to keep you from meeting the hiring manager! She is, in effect, the gatekeeper.

But once you get past the gate, be careful of what's on the other side.

1. The Stress Interview

Anyone who's been through one of these never forgets it. The stress interview is designed to cut through the veneer of pleasantries to the heart of the matter. To see what a candidate is really made of.

I was subjected to a stress interview before I'd ever heard of the technique—not the best way to prepare, believe me.

Several years ago, I applied for an editorial position at a major publishing company. I made it past the first hurdle, a screening interview conducted in the corporate office. Next, I was invited to come back to meet the director of personnel, Carrie. After greeting me pleasantly, Carrie led me back to her rather palatial office. We chatted for a few minutes as I settled in. Then everything changed. Suddenly, I was undergoing an interrogation—worthy of the secret police in a country on Amnesty International's Top Ten.

Assuming that I had been given good reviews by the first screening interviewer, I was shocked when Carrie began firing. First she questioned my credentials. Why, she wondered sarcastically, had I majored in liberal arts rather than something "practical." She demanded to know what in the world made me think that I could edit a magazine (even though I had been doing it quite well for years).

Each successive question skittered in a dizzying new direction. If the first question was about my work experience, the next launched into my fitness routine, and the next, my favorite movie.

Carrie's questions did exactly what I later discovered they were intended to do—they made me feel confused, fearful and hostile. I behaved badly, I admit. I answered most of her questions in monosyllables, avoiding her eyes.

Needless to say, I was not offered the job.

But I did learn some valuable lessons from Carrie that day:

- *Never let them see you sweat.* In other words, no matter how stressful the situation, stay calm. Never take your eyes from the interviewer. When he or she finishes asking a question, take a few seconds to compose yourself and then, and only then, answer.

- *Recognize the situation for what it is*. It is nothing more than an artificial scenario designed to see how you react under pressure. The interviewer probably has nothing against you personally.

- *Don't become despondent.* It's easy to think that the interviewer has taken a strong dislike to you and that your chances for completing the interview process are nil. That's not the case. The stress interview is designed to see if you will become depressed, hostile and flustered when the going gets tough.

• *Watch your tone of voice.* It's easy to become sarcastic during a stress interview, especially if you don't realize what the interviewer is up to.

2. The Situational Interview

"What would happen if everyone else called in sick and...?"

There's nothing quite like the terror of the hypothetical question. Especially when it is a product of the interviewer's rich imagination. We'll talk more about these devils in Chapter 9. But for now, know that the hypothetical question should start a red light flashing in your consciousness. It is your signal that you are about to undergo an increasingly popular type of interview—the situational interview.

The premise is sound. Present the candidate with situations that might, hypothetically, occur on the job in order to gauge the degree to which he or she demonstrates the traits that will lead to success.

But what's good for the interviewer is often deadly for the interviewee. You will have to devote a great deal of thought to each of these questions. If you find yourself caught in this snare, stay calm and use the homework you have already done on your personal inventory to untangle yourself.

3. The Behavioral Interview

The hypothetical is just too "iffy" for some interviewers. This breed is more comfortable staying in the realm of the known, so they will dig deep into your past experience hoping to learn more about how you have already behaved in a variety of on-the-job situations. Then they'll attempt to use this information to extrapolate your future reactions on this job.

How did you handle yourself in some really tight spots? What kinds of on-the-job disasters have you survived? Did you do the right thing? What were the repercussions of your decisions?

Be careful of what you say. Every situation you faced was unique in its own way, so be sure to let the interviewer in on specific limitations you had to deal with. Did you lack adequate staff? Support from management? If you made the mistake of plunging in too quickly, say so and admit that you've learned to think things through. Explain what you'd do differently the next time around.

That said, my advice would be to steer away from the specifics of a particular situation and emphasize the personal strengths and expertise you'd feel comfortable bringing to any challenge you're likely to face.

4. The Team Interview

Today's organizational hierarchies are becoming flatter. That means that people at every level of a company are more likely to become involved in a variety of projects and tasks—including interviewing you for the job you're after.

How does this happen? That depends on the company. The team interview can range from a pleasant conversation to a torturous interrogation. Typically you will meet a group, or "team," of interviewers around a table in a conference room. They may be members of your prospective department or a crosssection of employees from throughout the company who you can expect to work with at some time or other in your new position.

The hiring manager or someone from human resources may chair an orderly session of question-and-answer—or turn the group loose to shoot questions at you like a firing squad. When it's all over, you'll have to survive the assessment of every member of the group.

Some hiring managers consult with the group after the interviewer for a "reading" on your performance. Others determine their decision using group consensus. The good news is that you don't have to worry that the subjective opinion of just one person will determine your shot at the job. Say one member of the group thinks you "lacked confidence" or came across as "arrogant." Others in the group may disagree. The interviewer who leveled the criticism will have to defend his or her opinion to the satisfaction of the group—or be shot down.

A group of people is also more likely (but not guaranteed) to ask you a broader range of questions that may uncover and underline your skills and expertise. Just take your time—and treat every member of the team with the same respect and deference you would the hiring manager.

Level Two: The Hiring Interview

You've made it this far. But don't relax yet. Your first interview with the person who will manage your prospective position is not likely to be a walk in the park. You may be stepping out of range of the experience and interviewing talent of the human resources professional—into unknown territory.

And you could wander there for a while.

Why? Experienced interviewers are trained to stay in charge of the interview, not let it meander down some deadend, nonproductive track. There is a predictability to the way they conduct interviews, even when they wield different techniques.

A Little Knowledge is a Dangerous Thing

On the other hand, the hiring manager is sure to lack some or all of the screening interviewer's knowledge, experience and skill—making him or her an unpredictable animal.

The vast majority of corporate managers don't know what it takes to hire the right candidate. Few of them have had formal training in conducting interviews of any kind. To make things worse, most managers feel slightly less comfortable conducting the interview than the nervous candidate sitting across their desks from them!

For example, a manager might decide you are not the right person for the job, without ever realizing that the questions he or she asked were so ambiguous, or so off the mark, that even the perfect candidate could not have returned the "right" answer. No one monitors the performance of the interviewer. And the candidate cannot be a mind-reader. So more often than is necessary, otherwise perfectly qualified candidates are apt to walk out the door for good simply because the manager failed at the interview!

Foiling the Inept Interviewer

But that doesn't have to happen to you. You can—and should—be prepare to put your best foot forward, no matter what the manager who is interviewing for the job does or says. That begins with having the answers to 101 questions at the ready. But it doesn't stop there. Because the interviewer may not ask any of these questions.

What do you do then? In the chapters that follow, you'll see how you can give even the most dense of managers the feeling that you are the best person for the job.

Simply put, you're a step ahead of the game if you realize at the outset that managers who are interviewing to hire are after more than just facts about your skills and background. They are waiting for something more elusive to hit them, something they themselves may not be able to articulate. They want to feel that somehow you "fit" the organization or department.

Talk about a tough hurdle! But knowing what you're up against is half the battle. Rather than sit back passively and hope for the best, you can help the unskilled interviewer focus on how your unique skills can directly benefit—"fit"—the department or organization using a number of specific examples.

One word of caution. Don't come on so strong that you seem to be waging a campaign. You'll come off as overzealous and selfserving. You lose. Just keep quietly and confidently underlining the facts (your expertise) and enthusiastically showing (discovering together) how well these "puzzle pieces" seem to fit the job at hand.

That Certain Something

One afternoon, Alexander, my boss and the publishing director for the magazine I was running, asked me to stop by his office to meet a promising young candidate a friend had referred. "I know you don't have any positions open right now, Ron," he told me. "But could you take the time just to say hello?"

I was up to my ears with work, but I took a few moments to find out a little bit about Lynn. I asked her a few preliminary questions: Where she was working? What were her strengths? What she was looking for? I had planned to be out of there in five minutes.

But, somehow, we were still talking a half-hour later. By that time, I knew she was a terrific writer and editor. And I understood why she was thinking about making a move.

I still couldn't offer her a job. But she had impressed me so much in that informal meeting that when the managing editor spot opened up on my magazine a few months later, I didn't think twice. I called Lynn. After a more thorough and formal interview, she got the job.

What made Lynn such a winner? She displayed just those traits that I keep stressing, the traits employers are always looking for, no matter what the job description: confidence, enthusiasm, experience and dependability.

Your Outline of This Chapter

_____

_____

_____

_____

_____

_____

_____

_____

_____

_____

_____

_____

_____

_____

_____

_____

_____

_____

_____

_____

_____

_____

_____

_____

Take Notes

My Outline of This Chapter

State of Interviewing Today

Key: I= interview   IR= Interviewer
       E= employer   C = candidate

I. Overview
    A. IRs reluctant 2 lve anything 2 chance
    B. I gone » art 2 science.
    C. Many new I methods developed & used.
    D. I more challenge than ever
        1. Downsizing left fewer jobs, cost/hire up.
        2. Lawsuits up
        3. More competition
        4. Es looking 4 "perfect" Cs
            a. So + Is, + tests
            b. Different kinds of Is
II. Screening I
    A. W/ human resources
    B. Job: weed out Cs
    C. Will follow script
    D. Then 2 prof. I techniques
        1. Stress I
            a. Purpose: confuse/intimidate
            b. How handle?
                (1). Stay calm
                (2). Not personal
                (3). Don't get depressed/angry
        2. Situational I
            a. Hypothetical questions
            b. Require thought, stay calm, use personal
               inventory

3. Behavioral I
   a. Dig into experience
   b. Explain details, tell what do different
   c. Emphasize personal strengths/expertise
4. Team I
   a. Group interview, orderly or like firing squad
   b. Usually mean group input, even gp. decision
   c. Usually ask broader range of questions

III. Hiring I.
   A. Hiring mgr unpredictable IR
      1. Not prof IRs
      2. May B uncomfortable 2
   B. Dealing w/ inept IR
      1. Have answers ready
      2. IRs lking 4 "chemistry"
      3. Don't B 2 aggressive

IV. What Es lking 4
   A. Enthusiasm
   B. Confidence
   C. Experience
   D. Dependibility

Chapter Eleven

SOME NOTES ON ADD

We both fear and pity kids on illegal drugs. But we also must face and deal with what's happening to the 3 million-plus who are on a *legal* drug—Ritalin, the prescribed drug of choice for kids diagnosed with Attention Deficit Disorder (ADD), hyperactivity or the combination of the two (ADHD).

I could write a book on ADD, which seems to be the "diagnosis of choice" for school kids these days. Luckily, I don't have to. Thom Hartmann has already written an excellent one—***Attention Deficit Disorder: A Different Perception***—from which I have freely and liberally borrowed (with his permission) for this chapter.

I'm going to leave others to debate whether ADD actually exists as a clearly definable illness, whether it's the "catchall" diagnosis of lazy doctors, whether teachers are labeling kids as ADD to avoid taking responsibility for the students' poor learning skills, whether Ritalin is a miracle drug or one that is medicating creative kids into a conforming stupor.

All of these positions *have* been asserted, and, as hundreds of new kids are medicated every day, the debate about ADD is only likely to continue...and heat up.

That is not my concern in this book.

What I want to deal with here is the reality that many kids, however they're labeled, have severe problems in dealing with school as it usually exists. And to give them the advice they need—especially regarding note-taking—to contend with the symptoms that have acquired the label "ADD".

Some definitions, please

Just what is ADD? It's probably easiest to describe as a person's difficulty focusing on a simple thing for any significant period of time. People with ADD are described as easily distracted, impatient, impulsive and often seeking immediate gratitude. They often have poor listening skills and have trouble doing "boring" jobs (like sitting quietly in class or, as adults, balancing a checkbook). "Disorganized" and "messy" are words that also come up a lot.

Hyperactivity, on the other hand, is more clearly defined as restlessness, resulting in excessive activity. Hyperactives are usually described as having "ants in their pants." ADHD, the first category recognized in medicine some 75 years ago, is a combination of hyperactivity and ADD.)

According to the American Psychiatric Association, a person has ADHD if they meet eight or more of the following paraphrased criteria:

1. They can't remain seated if required to do so.

2. They are easily distracted by extraneous stimuli.

3. Focusing on a single task or play activity is difficult.

4. Frequently begin another activity without completing the first.
5. Fidgets or squirms (or feels restless mentally).
6. Can't (or doesn't want to) wait for his turn during group activities
7. Will often interrupt with an answer before a question is completed.
8. Has problems with chore or job follow-through
9. Can't play quietly easily.
10. Impulsively jumps into physically dangerous activities without weighing the consequences.
11. Easily loses things (pencils, tools, papers) necessary to complete school or work projects
12. Interrupts others inappropriately.
13. Talks impulsively or excessively.
14. Doesn't seem to listen when spoken to.

Three caveats to keep in mind: The behaviors must have started before age seven, not represent some other form of classifiable mental illness and occur more frequently than the average person of the same age.

Characteristics of people with ADD

Let's look at the characteristics generally ascribed to people with ADD in more detail:

Easily distracted—Since ADD people are constantly "scoping out" everything around them, focusing on a single item is difficult. Just try having a conversation with an ADD person while a television is on.

Take Notes

Short, but very intense, attention span—Though it can't be defined in terms of minutes or hours, anything an ADD person finds boring immediately loses their attention. Other projects may hold their rapt and extraordinarily intense attention for hours or days.

Disorganization—ADD children and adults are often chronically disorganized—their rooms are messy, their desk a shambles, their files incoherent. While people without ADD can certainly be equally messy and disorganized, they can usually find what they are looking for; ADDers *can't*.

Distortions of time-sense—ADDers have an exaggerated sense of urgency when they're working on something and an exaggerated sense of boredom when they have nothing interesting to do.

Difficulty following directions—A new theory on this aspect holds that ADDers have difficulty processing auditory or verbal information. A significant aspect of this difficulty is the very-common reports of parents of ADD kids who say their kids love to watch TV and hate to read.

Daydream—Or fall into depressions or mood-swings.

Take risks—ADDers seem to make faster decisions than non-ADDers. Which is why Thom Hartmann and Wilson Harrell, former publisher of *Inc.* magazine and author of ***For Entrepreneurs Only***, conclude that the vast majority of successful entrepreneurs probably have ADD! They call them "Hunters", as opposed to the more staid "Farmer" types.

Easily frustrated and impatient—ADDers do *not* beat around the bush or suffer fools gladly. They are direct and to-the-point. When things aren't working, "Do something!" is the ADD rallying cry, even if that something is a bad idea.

Why ADD kids have trouble in school

First and foremost, says Thom Hartmann, it's because schools are set up for "Farmers"—sit at a desk, do what you're told, watch and listen to the teacher. This is pure hell for the "Hunters" with ADD. The bigger the class size, the worse it becomes. Kids with ADD, remember, are easily distracted, easily bored, easily turned off, always ready to move on.

What should you look for in a school setting to make it more palatable to an ADD son or daughter? What can you do at home to help your child (or yourself)? Hartmann has some solid answers:

- *Learning needs to be project- and experience-based*, providing more opportunities for creativity and shorter and smaller "bites" of information. Many "gifted" programs offer exactly such opportunities. The problem for many kids with ADD is that they've spent years in non-gifted, Farmer-type classroom settings and may be labeled underachieving behavior problems, effectively shut out of the programs virtually designed for them! Many parents report that children diagnosed as ADD, who failed miserably in public school, thrived in private school. Hartmann attributes this to the smaller classrooms, more individual attention with specific goal-setting, project-based learning and similar methods common in such schools. These factors are just what make ADD kids thrive!

- *Create a weekly performance template* on which *both* teacher and parent chart the child's performance, positive and negative. "Creating such a larger-than-the-child system," claims Hartmann, "will help keep ADD children on task and on time.

- *Encourage special projects for extra credit*. Projects give ADDers the chance to learn in the mode that's most appropriate to them. They will also give such kids the chance to make up for the "boring" homework they sometimes simply can't make themselves do.

- *Stop labeling them "disordered"*—Kids react to labels, especially negative ones, even more than adults. Saying "you have a deficit and a disorder" may be more destructive than useful.

- *Think twice about medication,* but don't discard it as an option. Hartmann has a very real concern about the long-term side effects of the drugs normally prescribed for ADDers. He also notes that they may well be more at risk to be substance abusers as adults, so starting them on medication at a young age sends a very mixed message. On the other hand, if an ADD child cannot have his or her special needs met in the classroom, *not* medicating him or her may be a disaster. "The relatively unknown long-term risks of drug therapy," says Hartmann, "may be more than offset by the short-term benefits of improved classroom performance."

Specific suggestions about note-taking

Three aspects of ADDers that we discussed previously make it very difficult for them in note-taking situations, especially in a classroom setting: They're easily distracted, have a short attention-span and have difficulty processing auditory information. Which means even if they manage to remain interested, they may be distracted by anything else inside or outside the classroom. If they beat that, they may simply fail to process the lecture everyone else is hearing.

There are four key solutions to these problems. First, despite what I have written earlier in this book and in others, ADDers *should* tape record lectures. This will enable them to relisten and reprocess information they may have missed the first time around. (Students can also consider asking their professors for their own detailed outlines, notes or even typed-up lectures that they can duplicate. I have never heard of anyone asking for these, and I can see why professors wouldn't agree, but it's certainly worth a try!)

Second, rather than attempting to take notes using words— even the abbreviations and shorthand I've recommended— ADDers should instead utilize pictures, mapping, diagrams, etc. in lieu of outlines or "word" notes.

Third, they should also learn and practice the process of visualization. Anyone with ADD (or a parent of one) should realize that the mental imaging taught in many memory courses is precisely what will help an ADDer deal with this problem. Practice making visual pictures of things while having conversations; create mental images of lists of things to do; visualize yourself doing things you commit to. And practice paying attention when people talk to you. Listen carefully.

Fourth, joining a study group should be mandatory. A bright ADDer has a lot to add (pardon the pun) to any group, and access to the group's notes may well be life-saving.

Take Notes

INDEX

Take Notes